DAUGHTERS
OF THE KING
DAILY DEVOTIONALS
Volume 1

Table of Contents

A Special Note

"Do not despise these small beginnings" Zechariah 4:10, NLT.

♔

While seeking God in prayer, I heard Him say in a still small voice, "I want you to start a women's ministry and I want you to call it "Daughters of the King International Ministries." He told me to start by launching a daily devotional. I obeyed Him and wrote my first devotional. I then released it the very next day to the women on my email list, which were no more than 70 women at the time. Within three years we had a team of anointed writers and a devotional app that is now reaching hundreds of thousands of people around the world. To God be the glory.

I believe the secret to godly success is seeking the Lord and doing what He tells you—nothing more and nothing less.

It is good when you can say to God, "I did what you asked me to do, now what?"

After asking God "now what," we are instructed to continue expanding and advancing His kingdom in keeping with the mission He gave us of:

Inspiring Women Around the World

"Only ask, and I will give you the nations as your inheritance, the whole earth as your possession" Psalms 2:8, NLT.

Our devotionals are being used by God to inspire women globally. To make sure everyone is reached, we are working to create a translation of Daughters of the King Daily Devotionals in every language.

Praying For Revival Among Us

"Awake, O sleeper, and arise from the dead, and Christ will shine on you" Ephesians 5:14, ESV.

We believe the Spirit of God is a quickening spirit. He causes us to come alive and be awakened. With every devotional we release, we desire to awaken believers and help them run with God's plan for their lives.

Encouraging Unity

"I pray that they will all be one, just as you and I are one" John 17:21, NLT.

One day in prayer God said to me, "When you are unified, I will release blessings into your life. My people are not supporting each other like they should. They are too busy competing. There must be a spirit of unity." Daughters of the King is about uniting daughters of God from all over the world for one sole purpose, and that's to glorify the Lord. We are thankful to God that we are seeing this come to pass.

Thank You to our Devotional Writers

I want to sincerely thank our devotional writers: Sonja Thompson, Evelyn Suarez, Crystal Jewell, Almira Robinson, Torah Howard, Gabrielle Elisco, Angela Lewis, Ebony Hicks, Kirsi Karlsson, Dawn Stewart, Kathleen Watchinski, Samone Vail, Stella Boakye, Angela Curry, Kristina Fox, Nadolyn Dunigan, Crystal Marie Kamyszek aka "Cricket", Brenda Dawson, Jasmin Stankovic, Juanita Ortiz, Dumebi Jennifer Okwundu, Aly Hines and Tammy A. Phillips. Without your help, this devotional ministry wouldn't be where it is today.

To the one holding this book, thank you for reading Daughters of the King Daily Devotionals and for allowing God to minister to your heart through this ministry. We often hear how much our devotionals bless you, but you bless us more than you may ever know. I pray as you read through these pages, that God will enrich your soul and cause you to never be the same.

Kesha Trippett
DOTK Daily Devotionals Founder
and Contributing Writer

See and Be Radiant

"Lift up your eyes all around, and see; they all gather together, they come to you; your sons shall come from afar, and your daughters shall be carried on the hip. Then you shall see and be radiant; your heart shall thrill and exult, because the abundance of the sea shall be turned to you, the wealth of the nations shall come to you..." Isaiah 60:4-4, ESV.

Many times when we are faced with what seems like insurmountable circumstances. It is easy to sink into a pit of despair. However, God's promises are true (see 2 Corinthians 1:20), and His ways are perfect (see Psalms 18:30). God has never left you nor forsaken you (see Deuteronomy 31:8).

Faith is an act of submission. You have to choose to act in accordance to His Word and "Lift up your eyes", look at your situation, speak to it, and declare the Word of the Lord. Choose to speak life over your circumstance and declare that Lord of the

Breakthrough (see 2 Samuel 5:20) will allow you to "see and be radiant". When you don't know how to pray, pray God's Word and make it personal to your situation.

Here is example: If you take Zechariah 4:7 and make it personal to you it would be:

Nothing, not even a mighty mountain, will stand in my way; it will become a level plain before me! And I will shout: 'May God bless it! May God bless it!'"

Find a scripture that speaks to you and make it personal. If you will use His Word to speak life when you cannot see it, it will strengthen and encourage you until you can. Take time to dig deep in God's Word and find passages that reminds you to be strong, vigilant, and courageous in despair.

Post the scriptures in places where you go all the time, so you are surrounded with a covering of His promises. Choose today to ACT in faith, and walk in victory!

Prayer: *Father, speak to me today through your Word. Show me how to speak life over my circumstances. Right now, I am weak, and I need You. I surrender my will to your will. I ask you to guide me and quicken me when I speak anything other than faith. I trust you and I know you will bring breakthrough in my life. Amen*

A Special Prayer for You

ᕷ

Father God, I come before You on behalf of Your daughter who is reading this prayer right now. My heart can feel her pain. My heart can feel her need for You. I pray You will intervene in her life. I pray You cause her to see You in ways she's never seen. Cause her to know the depth of Your love for her. She belongs to You and are in the palm of Your hands. Nothing and no one can separate her from Your love. When life doesn't make sense and when it seems like it's too much to handle, remind her of who she is in You. Fill her with Your Holy Spirit and Your power. She is not the same woman she use to be. She has been made new in Christ. Help her to put on the new man and receive Your grace. I cover her in prayer right now and plead the protective blood of Jesus over her now. Let Your healing hands touch the deep places in her heart that have become cold and callous. You are her deliverer. Deliver her from the grip of the enemy and place her in Your beautiful Kingdom. Place her in Your perfect will for her life and flood her life with light. Give her supernatural peace. I pray You help her not try to earn anything You've given her freely, but to simply receive it. Download Your wisdom into her heart and be glorified in her life as she walks with You. In Jesus' name I pray, Amen.

"But you are a chosen people, a royal priesthood, a holy nation, God's special possession, that you may declare the praises of him who called you out of darkness into his wonderful light."
1 Peter 2:9, NIV

It's Not Over

*"The grass withers, the flower fades, but the word of
our God stands forever"*
Isaiah 40:8, NKJV.

♔

Today, there is a situation you might be facing. You have prayed and prayed, yet have not physically seen the hand of God in your situation. Sometimes it is hard to see the forest for the trees. Sometimes we just can't comprehend why things are taking so long to manifest. But my precious sister, know that God's timing is perfect. It's not over until God says it's over.

It might look impossible. From your view, there is just no way. Let me assure you today that our Father is stirring His pot of grace. In the spiritual realm, He is preparing hearts, adjusting people, opening doors, calling forth opportunities, lifting up a standard against the enemy, and coming on the scene like never before. The Lord delights in you. He desires for you to have the abundant life in Him. Your season is near. The devil is making it look like things will never change, but God says, "The change has already been made in Me. Things have already shifted in your favor. I have opened up the store gates of Heaven and I Am preparing a blessing you won't believe. Hold on My daughter, hold on. Draw your strength from Me. Keep looking up to Me from where your help comes from and get ready. Get ready! Get prepared to receive full manifestation of My glorious promises. Praise Me and rejoice in Me because it is coming to you!"

Prayer: *Hallelujah! Glory to God! Father, I am speechless. Thank you for speaking directly to my heart. Help me to keep my eyes and my mind stayed on You while You do just what You promised me. In Jesus' name. Amen.*

(Read Malachi 3:10; Isaiah 40:20-23: Psalm 145:3)

A message from God's heart for you.

⚜

"Just because you've never done something, doesn't mean you never will, and just because you've always done something, doesn't mean you always will. That Kingdom woman that you desire to be, that Kingdom level you desire to operate in, and that Kingdom that you desire to help advance, I put that desire in you and it's waiting for your discovery. All fear, doubt and unbelief was learned from the experiences you've had here in this earthly realm, but that's not who you really are. You really are My daughter and your true identity is in Christ. The real you is full of compassion, full of mercy, full of wisdom and affection for Me. Call on Me My beloved and precious daughter, call on Me and I will surely answer you and show you great and mighty things that you do not know. I will make you rich in experiences with Me. I will help you see who you are in Me and who I am in you. I delivered you from the power of darkness and have placed you in the Kingdom of My dear Son. No one can snatch you from My Hand. You are Mine and I am yours. My answer to you is Yes. Yes, you are that Kingdom woman you desire to be in Me. Yes, you will operate on that Kingdom level. Yes, you will advance My Kingdom like you never thought possible. Before you were formed in your mother's womb, I knew you and I called you. I will help you see your greatest potential. I say Yes."

Prayer: *My Father. My God. Thank You for speaking to me. You know where I am and what I need. I need You. Only You delivered and healed me. No man can take credit for what You did in me, and for that I give You everything. Be glorified in me. Love, Your Daughter.*

(Read Jeremiah 33:3; Colossians 1:13; Jeremiah 1:5)

Love will make you bold.

"So Jesus had compassion on them, and touched their eyes: and immediately their eyes received sight, and they followed him" Matthew 20:34, KJV.

꒰ꑇ꒱

So often we pray for God to give us boldness, to make us brave and courageous. It's not boldness we need. We need God to enlarge our hearts and fill us with His love.

When I first gave my life to the Lord, I prayed for boldness because I wanted to make a difference in my school and among my friends. But as I grew spiritually, my prayers changed. Instead of asking God for boldness, I began to pray for an enlarged heart, and from that place of prayer, there came the courage and boldness I longed for.

Love will make you bold. Love will make you tell someone the truth. Love will make you courageously stand in front of a group of people you don't know to share what God has revealed to you. Love will cause you to lay hands on the sick and believe God to heal them. Love will cause you to give food to the poor and sacrifice to help someone in need. Is not this what Jesus did? We call them miracles, but all Jesus was doing was loving people. He was moved with compassion and it produced countless miracles.

Not many miracles are being seen due to a lack of love. The Bible says, because of the increase in wickedness, the love of most people will grow cold (see Matthew 24:12). Say, "NOT ME!!"

Say it again, "NOT ME! God please enlarge my heart. Soften every hardened place in my heart. Change the temperature of my heart from cold to blazing hot for you. Use me to produce countless miracles for your glory alone. Start with the miracle in me. In the name of Jesus. Be glorified in me. Love, Your daughter."

(Read Matthew 9:36; Psalm 145:8; 1 John 4:18; 2 Timothy 1:7)

Receive the tiny crumbs of purpose.

"But the path of the righteous is like the light of dawn, which shines brighter and brighter until full day"
Proverbs 4:18, ESV.

♔

God's specific purpose and plan for your life can't be seen all at once. He reveals more and more as you go along. It's like eating the tiny crumbs on the floor that gets bigger and bigger in size until we reach the bigger, much larger, cookie. That's similar to how our purpose works. We follow Him in the smallest commands first. Doing the things we already know to do, until He gives more light and instructions. Some people might never discover their big cookie of a purpose because they won't stoop down to eat the crumbs that lead to it.

An old friend of mine who I had

known for many years, would tell me over and over again, "You have a gift of encouragement." I didn't think anything of it. I actually thought it was odd that she called encouragement a spiritual gift. But she would keep telling me until one day I figured if I'm able to encourage people in a gifted way, why not let it work for me. So I began to look for opportunities and creative ways to encourage others.

What people tell you over and over again about yourself is an indicator of what you're good at. It is an indicator of your purpose. You are happiest when you are doing what you were created to do. Your joy level may be at an all time low and you're fighting hard not to cave in to the pressure. Cave in to God instead. You have nothing to lose. Let Him use you to the fullest extent. Receive the tiny crumb of purpose He's already revealed and trust Him every step of the way to reveal more. There is an expected end. There is a bigger plan and purpose far greater than you can ever imagine. Do the little things very well. Put your heart and your all into the little things and look for more around the bend.

Prayer: *Father God, thank You. You are so good. I love you more than anything. Keep on teaching me by Your Spirit. Keep on helping me trust your plans for me. I humble myself and I stoop down and receive the tiny crumbs, the small instructions. Lead me and help me get to that place you thought of when you were forming me in my mother's womb. I want to please You more than anything. Love, Your daughter.*

(Read Jeremiah 29:11-13)

God wants you to be available.

"Let your light so shine before men, that they may see your good works, and glorify your Father which is in heaven" Matthew 5:16, KJV.

One afternoon while leaving the grocery store, I noticed a woman limping slowly to her car. I looked at her foot and it appeared as though she had just had surgery. She wore a special shoe. So I asked if I could pray for her. I said, "Hi ma'am, I know you don't know me, but would you mind if I pray for your foot? I believe God loves to heal people." She looked at me and said, "Yes." I promised her that I wouldn't pray a long drawn out prayer. So I touched her leg and prayed, "Father, I pray for my sister. I believe you care when we're in pain. I pray you heal her foot Father God and take away all the pain. In Jesus' name, Amen." With tears in her eyes, she thanked me and asked if she could give me a hug. "Of course," I told her. I then hugged her and went on my way...thankful to God for using me to bless someone.

God wants you to be available to Him, ready and willing to be used by Him at any given moment. You may not know enough to be a Bible scholar, but you do know Jesus and what He has done for you, and that's enough to be dangerous to the kingdom of darkness and highly useful in the Kingdom of God!

Prayer: *Father God, I thank You for speaking so clearly to me. I cast my cares on you because I know you care for me. I make myself available to you to work through me. I am ready and willing Father. Show your love through me and shine your amazing light. Help me brighten someone's day. In Jesus' name, Amen.*

(Read 2 Timothy 4:2)

The Endless Staircase

*"See, I am doing a new thing! Now it springs up; do
you not perceive it? I am making a way in the
wilderness and streams in the wasteland"*
Isaiah 43:19, NIV.

⚜

Throughout my walk with Jesus, I have
experienced many ups and downs. There
were days when I felt as though I was in
perfect sync with God, and others where I
felt nothing but condemnation for my
shortcomings.

Every time I would mess up, I set
myself back. I imagined myself on an
endless staircase with no destination or end
point. In my mind, I kept heading upward
on the good days, the days I felt holy, and
filled with a heart of praise and
thanksgiving.

Then, on the days I didn't feel so
great about myself or knew I missed the
mark and blew it yet again, I imagined I fell

down a considerable flight of stairs. One step forward on the good days, ten steps backward on the bad days.

I felt unworthy, would beat myself up over my mistakes and thought I had to serve my "time-out" and perform better before I could come into the presence of my Savior again. This is a nuclear defense of the devil. When we mess up, his condemnation and guilt sweep in to put a wall between us and our Father. But what does Jesus do? He makes all things new. He hung on that cross so that when we fall short, we can receive His sweet forgiveness. He is ready to forgive us, before we even come before Him to ask for His mercy yet again.

Sister, there is now no condemnation to you because you are in Christ Jesus (see Romans 8:1). That mistake you made, He casts it as far as the east is from the west, and He remembers it no more (Psalm 103:12; Hebrews 8:12). The sin you committed, He washed in His blood. The mess you made of things, He has made new and is creating a divine purpose.

He is saying to you today, "I will carry you forward. Stop punishing yourself. The price has already been paid. I carried away your shame, your sins, your insecurities. I rescued you from the power of darkness and placed you in my Kingdom. You are mine and I'm taking you to higher ground now."

Prayer: *Father, I thank You for your endless mercies and Your forgiveness. Lord, I ask You to forgive me of my sins and the times I have failed You. Help me to put the past behind me as You already have. Help me to stop punishing myself, and step into Your righteousness that You have given me through Your finished work. Carry me through, Jesus. I welcome Your presence to fill me, and heal every part of me that is broken. In Jesus name, Amen.*

(Read Isaiah 46:4; 1 Peter 2:24; Colossians 1:13)

Put Your Hands in His

*"Then Jesus spoke to them again, saying, "I am the
light of the world. He who follows Me shall not
walk in darkness, but have the light of life"*
John 8:12, NKJV.

ωω

One morning my youngest son came to me
and said, "Mommy, I have a surprise for
you." He wanted me to close my eyes and
hold his hand so he could lead me. So I did.
I had to trust he would not let me fall, run
into a wall or step on anything on the floor.
But as I walked with him, I could feel him
moving and kicking things out of my way.
He wanted me to get to his surprise without
any harm. When we arrived, he shouted,
"Surprise!"

The Lord deals with us in the same
way. He reveals to our heart that He has
something in store for us—an expected end.
All He requires is that we put our hands in
His and let Him lead us. What we don't

know is He is constantly moving things out of our way that could potentially harm us.

Maybe you're walking by faith, and you're hoping God won't let you fall, won't let you run into a wall or step in any situation that could bring you harm. Maybe you have entrusted your entire spiritual well-being into God's care like never before, and you are hoping God will do what He said He'll do. My sister, He will. If you keep walking with the Lord and letting Him lead you, you will arrive on time to His expected end.

Prayer: *Thank You Father God for revealing to my heart that You have something in store for me. I put my hand in Yours, and I trust You to lead me wherever You would have me go. I know You love me and have my best interest at heart. I know You won't let me fall. Thank You for moving people and things out of my way that are not good for me. I trust You. In Jesus' name, Amen.*

As I Have Loved You

"...love one another, as I have loved you."
John 15:12

ꞵ

Take a moment and think about how God has loved you. As much as you want to stay angry and resentful, or as much as you want to be impatient and give up on people who are trying to do better, remember how God has loved you. Has He stayed angry with you? Has He held on to your past mistakes? Has He been impatient with your growth and development? Has He ever disowned and disinherited you? Has He ever not loved you? The answer to all of these questions is an emphatic, "no". He has been faithful even when you've been faithless.

When you feel empty and incapable of loving others, it's an indicator that you aren't receiving God's love for yourself. Those who struggle with forgiving others, struggle with receiving God's total forgiveness in their own lives.

The Spirit of the Lord is saying..."As I have loved you Daughter, love each other. As I have forgiven you, forgive each other. As I've been patient with you, be patient with each other. As I've strengthened you, strengthen each other. As I've prayed for you, pray for each other."

When we see the sun, we expect to see its light and feel its warmth. When we see a believer in whom the Spirit of God dwells, we expect to see God's light and feel the warmth of His love.

Prayer: *Father God, thank You for speaking directly to my heart about Your love. I am deeply grateful for how You have loved me. I receive Your love and I pray You help me show it to others today. When I feel empty of love, help me remember to come to you and be filled to the overflow. I pray Your love is seen and felt through my life. In Jesus' name, Amen.*

(Read John 13:34; 1 Corinthians 13)

God only desires to bless you.

"Trust in and rely confidently on the Lord with all your heart and do not rely on your own insight or understanding. In all your ways know and acknowledge and recognize Him, and He will make your paths straight and smooth [removing obstacles that block your way]"
Proverbs 3:5-6, Amplified.

⚜

For the past few days I've heard God whisper to my heart, "Don't lean to your own understanding." It's as though He is re-teaching me this truth. While wondering what to do about a situation, I said, "Lord, I don't know what to do." He then told me to make a phone call, and when I did, that one phone call led to God's favor.

So often we rely on our understanding and the information we've gathered, and we fall short of God's blessings. We must know that God cares about every detail of our lives. He cares about everything that concerns us and wants to lead us to the blessing He has waiting for us. He wants us to walk in His favor, not just experience it every now and then. But it's up to us to follow His wisdom, His whispers, and His peace. It's up to us to not lean on our own understanding, but listen to Him.

He only desires to bless you.

Prayer: *Father God, thank You for giving me a deeper understanding of Your heart for me. You love me and only desire to bless me. You want me to walk in Your favor everyday of my life. Forgive me for every time I leaned on my own understanding. Help me understand more fully this truth. Help me pay attention to Your whispers to my heart and follow You. I want Your results, not my own. I thank You, In Jesus' name, Amen.*

(Read Jeremiah 29:11-13; James 1:5)

Saturate Yourself in Scripture

"Be diligent to present yourself approved to God, a worker who does not need to be ashamed, rightly dividing the word of truth"
2 Timothy 2:15, NKJV.

♔

It is important that our prayer life, our responses, our words, and thought life become saturated with God's Words found in the Bible. When a friend or family member comes to us with an issue, do we tell them what we think? Or do we direct them to what the Lord says in the Bible? Each day, make it a daily habit to spend time in the Word of God.

There are several rewards for giving God's Word our full and undivided attention. It will:

- Convert our soul and make us wise (see Psalm 19:7)

- Enlighten our darkness or ignorance (see Psalm 18:28)
- Nourish us and help us grow spiritually (see 1 Peter 2:2)
- Guide us through life (see Psalm 119:105)
- Help purify our hearts (see Hebrews 4:12)
- Minister life to us and to those around us (see John 6:63)
- Help us become more like Jesus (see 2 Corinthians 3:18)
- Renew our minds and change our thinking (see Romans 12:2)
- Teach us how to live right (see 2 Timothy 3:16)
- Equip us to fulfill God's purpose for our lives (see 2 Timothy 3:17)
- And the list goes on...

The good life we desire is found in a deeper relationship with God's Word. One that goes from simply knowing what the Bible says to applying it in our lives, letting it become our bottom-line that settles every issue in our hearts and minds.

Prayer: *Father God, I thank you for giving me wisdom, knowledge and understanding of your Word. I pray you deepen my relationship with Your Word and cause it to change my life and the lives of those around me. In Jesus name, Amen.*

(Read Psalms 119)

What it means to worship God.

"But a time is coming and is already here when the true worshipers will worship the Father in spirit [from the heart, the inner self] and in truth; for the Father seeks such people to be His worshipers"
John 4:23, Amplified.

♔

The Samaritan woman expressed to Jesus,"our fathers worshipped in this mountain, but the Jews worship in Jerusalem." There had been racial and religious tension between the Samaritans and Jews for years. Jesus gave a clear and concise response, "the hour will come and now is when the true worshippers will worship God neither in this mountain nor at Jerusalem, but they will worship Him in spirit and in truth."

To worship is to crouch, to bow, to reverence and honor. In this text, Jesus is emphasizing the kind of worship our Father God is looking for. He is looking for those who are crouched and bowed down in their hearts to Him and His truth. We can't bow down at the altar, but we are not bowed to how He instructs us to treat our sister or brother. We can't bow in worship and not bow in obedience to His command to forgive. We can't bow in worship and not bow to adhering to the laws of the land. We have to be careful not to worship the act of worship itself.

God is looking for such a person to worship Him from the heart and in obedience. He has given us His Spirit to teach us and lead us into all truth. It is up to us to humble ourselves to the truth He reveals to our hearts. When we do, we are worshipping Him and will get His results!

Prayer: *Father God, I thank You for giving me understanding. I humble myself right now to You and Your will. Forgive me for all pride and rebellion in my heart. I receive Your love and forgiveness. I bow down in my heart to You and Your truth. I reverence You Lord. Take control of my life and my heart. I want Your results. Not my own. In Jesus' name, Amen.*

(Read John 4:15-26; John 16:13)

Praise is an expression of faith.

"Let everything that has breath and every breath of life praise the Lord! Praise the Lord! (Hallelujah!)"
Psalms 150:6, Amplified

♔

One meaning of "praise" is to shine; to make a show; to boast; to be (clamorously) foolish; to rave; and to celebrate. The Bible says, "Let everything that has breath praise (shine, make a show, boast, be clamorously foolish, rave, and celebrate) the Lord!"

I love my husband and how he praises God. He has no problem praising, running, jumping, shouting and leaping. When he dances for the Lord, instead of standing at a distance feeling embarrassed, I jump right in with him. He looks like he's doing the funky chicken and I look like I'm killing bugs on the floor, but we don't care. We love to praise God and be clamorously foolish! We have discovered the power of praise!

I remember one time we moved into a new home and had no furniture. Instead of complaining, we called our four young children into our empty living room, and explained that we were going to praise God as a family. So we shouted, lifted our voices and praised God with everything we had. It was awesome! Two weeks later, our living room was full of quality furniture that we didn't have to pay a lot for.

God honors us when we honor Him. He loves the sound of our voices. He loves the sound of our steps on the floor and the clap of our hands. He lives in our praises!

Prayer: *Father God, You are my God and I praise You now. You are good and worthy of my praise. You are my Savior and an awesome Father to me. Thank You Lord! I know You have my life in Your hands, so I praise You! Let me be a walking celebration for You! In Jesus' Name, Amen.*

God is making you into a wise woman!

"For God did not give us a spirit of timidity or cowardice or fear, but [He has given us a spirit] of power and of love and of sound judgment and personal discipline [abilities that result in a calm, well-balanced mind and self-control]"
2 Timothy 1:7, Amplified

Listen...

You may have messed up more times than you can count, but if the only smart decision you ever made so far was to give your life to the Lord, you are doing great!!! Before you beat yourself up over the unwise decisions you've made, praise the Lord that you got one thing right! You were smart enough to receive Jesus! That's something to smile about.

Look at the good and not the bad. Look at what you've done right, instead of what you've done wrong. Let joy rise in your heart instead of regret over past mistakes you can't do anything to change. Be encouraged as you go through the process of learning how to be a wise woman for God glory!

Say out loud with me, *"God is making me into a wise woman! I ask God to forgive my mistakes and I rest in knowing I am forgiven. I receive God's love, His mercy and His grace. I move forward and I am made stronger and wiser from every wrong decision. God is increasing me in wisdom and in stature. I am increasing in favor with God and with man. I have soundness of mind and the ability to make sound decisions, not fear-based decisions, or emotional decisions, or impulsive decisions, but sound decisions that I will be pleased with tomorrow, and that please God. I'm not stupid! I'm not crazy! I'm not irresponsible! I'm not an underachiever! I'm an overcomer through Jesus Christ! I love God's word and I will walk in His wisdom and His grace. In Jesus' name!"*

(Read Proverbs 2:7; James 1:5; 1 Corinthians 1:30; Luke 2:52)

He can use you, no matter what.

*"I have no husband," she replied. Jesus said to her,
"You are right when you say you have no husband.
The fact is, you have had five husbands, and the
man you now have is not your husband. What you
have just said is quite true"*
John 4:17-18, NIV.

I gave my life to the Lord in my early adulthood, but that did not prevent me from making some gruesome mistakes in my life, especially in relations to men. I have divorced not once, but twice, both of which have not been my proudest moments. It has caused me to measure myself to those fortunate ones, who have had more sense than me in their lives. I felt belittled, like I failed and was basically damaged goods in the eyes of the Lord. I felt like someone with a bright future, but who stumbled greatly and was now doomed to live the rest of my life as an under achiever and snubbed.

The Lord began to talk to me about the woman at the well of Sykar. She too had many men in her life and was living with one who she was not married to. He reminded me how she met Jesus on the hottest time of the day. Feeling thirsty, ashamed to meet any other villagers and most likely feeling belittled, failed and like damaged goods. God told me that He knows what we have gone through in our lives and that He is not seeing us as little, failed or damaged. We don't have to be born-again Christians for decades without having made any mistakes, in order for Him to use us in a powerful way.

Just as He used the woman in the well of Sykar to minister to the whole village, He can use you to reach a multitude of people for His glory. All you need to do is to be honest in the presence of the Lord, not hiding anything. He sees it anyway. Be honest and thirsty for Him.

Your experiences are what makes you

who you are now. And what you are now makes you able to reach those people that the Lord has set before you.

Prayer: *Father God, thank You that You see us through the blood of Jesus, whole and made righteous through Jesus. I thank You that You are able to use us even in the middle of our twisted circumstances and with all our faults. I thank You that we don't have to measure ourselves to others, just to be in Your presence. Thank You for the freedom to simply be who we are in Christ. In Jesus name, Amen.*

A real sister won't judge you.

"Then you will know the truth, and the truth will set you free"
John 8:32, NIV

ꙥ

After opening up about an issue that I had held onto for fear of being judged or preached at, a friend told me, "Why are you acting like you're alone? You're not alone! I deal with the same thing and God is working on me too." That blessed me and was not the response I thought I would hear. We then talked further about our fears and insecurities, and by the end of the conversation we were both laughing, crying and bringing our hearts to the Lord in prayer. It was a beautiful moment. If I would have closed my heart from sharing honestly with her, I would have missed an opportunity to grow closer with my sister and dear friend.

The closeness you desire in your relationships is found in your openness and honesty. Be careful not to assume that your sister in Christ will respond negatively to your pain or problems. A real sister won't judge you or put you down. She'll provide love and encouragement. She'll remind you that she is also still being conformed to the image of Jesus and are being worked on just like you.

Be a real sister to someone, and let someone be a real sister to you.

Prayer: *I praise You Father God and I thank You for speaking directly to my heart. I know I'm not alone in the things I face. I come against pride and I humble myself now. I receive Your grace and truth. Thank you that I don't have to fear opening to You and those You've placed in my life. Help me to be a real sister and show me how to let others be a real sister to me. In Jesus' name, Amen.*

(Read Romans 8:29; Ephesians 2:4)

God's got you!

"For God did not give us a spirit of timidity or cowardice or fear, but [He has given us a spirit] of power and of love and of sound judgment and personal discipline [abilities that result in a calm, well-balanced mind and self-control]."
2 Timothy 1:7, NKJV.

࿐

Honestly, I don't know what's scarier, running from God or being in a new place with Him I've never been before. But He is faithful to calm my fears and whisper in my ear, "I got you!"

Hear this short, but powerful word from the Lord whispering to you, "I got you!"

You may be in a place you've never been before, but the Lord's got you. You must believe that you were made for this. For this cause you were born. God wouldn't help you get to a place of victory and then leave you. He's there to help you go from glory to glory and from faith to faith. He got you! You may feel afraid, but God's got you! Let His perfect love drive all the fear away. He loves you and He loves the people He will reach through you.

Love is the combatant of fear. It is impossible to be full of God's love and full of fear at the same time. Be reminded of God loves as you continue to walk into those dark places none would dare to go. Be reminded of God's love as you stand in a new place you've never seen. Be reminded of God's love as you stand before people you've never met. You are carrying God's light of love like a glowing torch and God is with you and will lead you.

Prayer: *Hallelujah! Father God I praise You. You know exactly what I need and when I need it. I feel afraid, but fear is not me. I put on Christ and I trust You got me. In Jesus' name, Amen.*

(Read 1 John 4:18; Colossians 3:10; Ephesians 6:10-18; Romans 13:14)

You're the oil, they're the vinegar and God is the soap.

"Above all, clothe yourselves with love, which binds us all together in perfect harmony"
Colossians 3:14, NLT.

ﮐ

While trying to tell my daughter how to handle a bully at school, I told her, "Maybe she's going through problems at home and need a friend to talk to. You can tell her if she ever wants to talk, you're there." To which my daughter responded, "I did, and she told me to mind my own business!" Then she said, "I'm just going to leave her alone until she cools off."

Have you ever met someone that was difficult to get along with? Maybe it's someone in the work environment, in your home, school, church, etc. You try everything, but they insist on being impossible to talk to, work with, and befriend.

When it comes to oil and vinegar, they don't mix. We find the only thing that can cause them to mix is an emulsifier. It is the outside agent that contains special compounds that wrap around the molecules in oil and causes them to bond with the water molecules in vinegar. For example, soap and egg yolk are both well-known emulsifiers, used to bring two very different substances together.

It's not in our own natural ability to be patient and forbearing with difficult people. We need an outside Agent. God's love is the great emulsifying agent that wraps around our hearts helping us do what we can't naturally do on our own. God's love will help you be wise and understanding when it comes to dealing with others. You're the oil, they're the vinegar and God is the soap.

Prayer: *Lord, I need You and I humble myself*

under Your mighty hand. Help me be understanding and patient with others, just as You are patient and understanding with me. Fill my heart with Your love and teach me how to love the same way. In Jesus' name I pray, Amen.

Passion is created in prayer.

I never envisioned myself being a first lady or a preacher for that matter. So when I met my husband who dreamed of pastoring a church one day, I questioned our compatibility right from the start. I told God, "I can't be what he will need me to be." I was a free flowing creative spirit who hated to feel boxed in. I was planning on becoming a famous painter and a business owner one day and ministry was nowhere near my life's pursuit. But God knows us better than we know ourselves. And with every purpose He gives us, He provides the passion, the anointing, the grace and the wisdom necessary to fulfill that particular assignment.

While in prayer, He began to give me a heart for pastor wives. I would find myself praying for them and my heart was enlarged for these precious daughters of God who give so much without asking anything in return. It was then that God birthed within me a passion for ministering to women.

Passion is created in prayer. God enlarges our hearts and causes our will to align with His will. He opens our eyes to see problems and how He is going to use us to solve them. It is a beautiful thing! While you may not be called to be a pastor's wife, trust that the Lord will give you the passion for what He has called you to do. He will equip you and cause all grace to abound toward you!

Prayer: *Father, thank You for speaking to my heart. I pray that You bless Your precious daughters throughout the world who are serving alongside their husband's in ministry. It is not an easy task, but Your grace won't fail them. As for me, Lord I trust that You know what is best for my life. Shape me and mold me into the woman You would have me to be. In Jesus Name, Amen.*

Do not be anxious about your life.

"Therefore I tell you, do not be anxious about your life,..." Matthew 6:25, ESV.

Your life is in God's hands. You can't control how He blesses you; all you must know is that He will. You don't know how He will meet your needs; all you must know is that He will. You don't know how He is going to get you from where you are right now to where He wants you to be in life. All you must know is that you've prayed, and He's heard you. It is His timing, His plan, His perfect will that is in effect for you.

When you stop trying to figure out how and when, you will be able to rest in His immense love and receive His grace that is apportioned to you today. Anxiety builds in our hearts when we concern ourselves with things beyond our control. God's grace builds in our lives when we walk in what He has set in front of us today.

Prayer: *Heavenly Father, I ask that you touch my heart. I have been anxious about many things, and I'm sorry. I receive your peace and comfort right now. I acknowledge your presence in my life. Thank you for being with me and for caring so much for me. You are my God; I have no reason to worry. I have no reason to be all worked up. I know you will take care of me. As I cast my cares on you, I ask that you help others to see how good you are and cause them to receive your love in their hearts so they too can be anxious for nothing. In the name of Jesus, Amen.*

(Read Matthew 6:25-34)

A message from God's heart for you.

ⱳ

"You have laid the hurting hearts of women at My feet. You have said pick them up and bring them to the cross for Me. For they are weak, and when you were weak I held you close and never let you go. For I made you for this purpose. You DO have a calling on your life. You DO have a purpose. You will move out and become who I designed you to be. I am going to use you to change hearts for Me. It has been your destiny. The loneliness and regret, the anguish and the torment, the abandonment and rejection, the loss and desertion, the tears you cried alone, the fears you fought alone, they will not be wasted. Your faith has been tested, and these will be your weapons in distress. You will remember how far I have brought you, how much I have taught you, and you will carry with you a badge of compassion that far exceeds your own ration. Because there are others in this world who have only tasted defeat and deceit, it is now your job to go out and meet them head on. Speak the truth in love. Tell them to hold on, hold onto hope, hold onto faith, to just wait and taste and see that the Lord is good! Show them how to take refuge in Me. Show them there is joy there in Me. Represent me well. Don't enlist your soul to Hell. Speak Heavenly words of truth and love and I will set you far above and set you and yours apart. I will overwhelm you with My love and hold you close to My heart. I have chosen you to become a contributing saint. Don't look away. Don't pretend to faint. I use the foolish things of the world to stump the wise, and thunder My truth to blinded eyes! There are those who can't see it, those who can't feel it, but to Me they still listen, they are still trying to hear it, attempting to hear a word of clarity amongst the fear, strife and tragedy. Words matter. Place them on the table before you on a platter of love and affection. Throw away condemnation and rejection. Rid your judgment and your hate. My Word is the key to your freedom, and your words will resonate into the caverns of death and darkness, filth and disease, anguish and hopelessness, despair and greed, remorse and regret, unforgiveness and hate. It is your time. Time to state that My Love in fact gives life and health back, healing and hope to those hanging by a rope. It gives purpose and forgiveness and righteousness for those who have been lost in prideful selfishness, without condemnation or punishment. I will replenish your life and will restore hope and love. I have set those apart who place Me above all other names. No more playing games. It is time for Kingdom business.. It is time to disciple and witness. I will make it so, says the Lord."

(Read Isaiah 61:1-3; 1 Corinthians 1:27; Isaiah 62:12; John 15:16)

A Special Prayer for You

Lord, I pray for your daughter who is reading this that you make her love increase and overflow for others as your love does for us. That you strengthen her heart so that she will be holy and blameless in your presence when our Lord Jesus Christ comes. Prepare for not only her but for her loved ones a path to come to Jesus and be made holy and blameless. Remove the stumbling blocks of this world planted by our enemy. Let the Holy Spirit fall upon her, that the veils be removed from not only her eyes and heart but her loved ones too. Let your mercy be for her in times of trouble when she stands alone for you, let her be reminded in your presence that you are with her and she is never truly alone, that your spirit dwells within her as her guide during these days of preparation for eternity. Thank you Jesus for your suffering and the gift of the Holy Spirit that aides your daughter in this world. She is your daughter and an heir to your kingdom. Help her to find joy and rejoice in her sufferings as she waits for you as you have waited for her. Let your power and truth be her strength and rest when she grows weary. Command your angels to guard her path and let your hand be against the enemy and your rod and staff be her comfort. You are her King, her refuge, and her Shepherd and I pray she will fear no evil. I declare the spirit that you've given her is not timid but of love, power, and a sound mind. Raise up both her and her loved ones and make them soldiers in your army, in Jesus' Name, Amen!

(Read Psalm 91; Psalm 23; 2 Peter 3:9; 2 Timothy 1:7; Matthew 18:6; John 14)

Healing takes place when we're truthful.

"Behold, you delight in truth in the inward being, and you teach me wisdom in the secret heart"
Psalms 51:6, ESV.

༒

My husband said something very wise to me while I was feeling emotional one day over a situation that occurred years ago. He said, "Don't pretend to be somewhere you are not, because pressure will prove where you really are." Those words have stayed with me.

Healing takes place when we're truthful. We can find healing in saying, "This is where I am right now. Yes, I still have faith in God, but this is where I am right now and I need your prayers and continued support."

Maybe you're still getting over the death of

someone or something, and you're trying to pretend that you're fine. Know that God knows you daughter. He knows where you truly are, and He knows how to get you where you need to be in life. Let God continue to minister healing to every deep wound. Let Him show you that those who genuinely love you won't mind you crying over something that happened years ago. And most importantly, let God help you to keep moving forward as He heals you completely and makes you whole.

Prayer: *Father God, I thank You for speaking to me. You know where I am right now and how challenging it has been. Help me not to pretend. I receive Your love and I receive Your comfort. I receive Your peace of mind and heart that's only found in You. I love You Lord. Heal every deep wound and fill every gaping hole that's been left in me. Help me be honest with You and with those who love me. In Jesus name, Amen.*

(Read Psalms 147:3; John 8:32)

You are being deeply rooted.

"As you therefore have received Christ Jesus the Lord, so walk in Him, rooted and built up in Him and established in the faith, as you have been taught, abounding in it with thanksgiving"
Colossians 2:6-7,NKJV.

Even though we are rooted and grounded in our knowledge of God, the enemy stops at nothing to try to uproot us. He quickly finds, however, that it is not an easy task.

Deep down there are things that we know. Deep down we know there is a God and that He loves us. Deep down we know that He will never leave us nor forsake us. Deep down we know that He has chosen us for His divine purposes and plans. Deep down we know that we are redeemed by the precious blood of Jesus and have been made new.

This is what being rooted and grounded means—holding on with everything we have to what we know deep down.

It doesn't matter what the enemy is trying to do, all that matters is what Jesus has already done on the cross!

Let us not uproot and give up! We must hold on and become even more rooted and grounded, and fully convinced of God's love. We must let His words permeate our heart and soul to the very core of who we are. When we do this, we will see that the enemy will not be able to win in our lives.

Through Jesus Christ, we are victorious! God is greater than anything we will ever face in this life and with His help we can do all things!

Prayer: *Father God, I know You are with me and that You love me. I know You are bigger than anything I'm facing right now. Establish me in Christ. Be glorified in my life and show everyone around me that You are my God! In Jesus' name, Amen.*

Praying God's Word

Have you ever needed to pray for someone, but the words just wouldn't come? I was having one of those moments, when the Lord took me into Psalm 1-6, where I found heartfelt prayers written by King David and other writers. Here are prayers from Psalms that you can pray for your loved ones.

For prosperity:

Thank you LORD, that _____'s delight is on the law of the LORD, and on his law _____ meditates day and night. _____ is like a tree planted by streams of water, which yield its fruit in season and whose leaf does not whither. Whatever _____ does prospers, in Jesus Name (see Psalm 1:2-3)!

For protection:

Thank you LORD that you are a shield around _____, O LORD, you bestow glory on _____ and lift up his head, in Jesus Name (see Psalm 3:3)!

In the name of Jesus, away from _____, all you who do evil, for the LORD has heard his weeping. The LORD has heard his cry for mercy; the LORD accepts his prayer. All _____'s enemies will be ashamed and dismayed; they will turn back in sudden disgrace (see Psalm 6:8-10).

In intercession:

LORD, how long will _____ turn your glory into shame? How long will he love delusions and seek false gods? Lord, I pray that _____ will know that you have set him apart for yourself; and I thank you that you, O LORD will hear _____ when he calls to You, in Jesus Name (see Psalm 4:2-3)!

Thank you LORD, that in his anger, _____ will not sin; when he is on his bed, he will search his heart and be silent, in Jesus Name (see Psalm 4:4)!

Prayer: *Lord God, thank you that your Word is powerful! Thank you, that when I don't know how to pray, you intercede on my behalf. Thank you for taking me to your Word! I believe the word I've prayed won't return void, but will accomplish all that I sent it out to do. In Jesus' name, Amen!*

You are Worth It

"But God commendeth his love toward us, in that, while we were yet sinners, Christ died for us."
Romans 5:8

♔

One evening, my son told me that he would kill himself. I grabbed him by his shirt and pulled him close to me. I wanted a memory to be etched in his mind forever if that thought was to ever return. I wanted him to remember my plea, my face, my love, my hand holding his shirt. So pulling him to me, I said, "Would you kill your sister?" He cried with tears in his eyes and tears in mine, "No". I continued, "Would you kill your brother?" He cried, "No." "Would you kill me?" I asked. He replied, "No." "So why would you kill you? You are worth living too."

We then hugged tightly and I went into my room, closed the door and cried. I had attempted to take my life years prior, but God rescued me, and here I was trying to convince my son that his life was worth living. In that moment, God comforted my heart and said, "Yes, you are worth it."

You may not see your worth, but God does. He does. He does. He does. Before you were born, God was thinking about how the sacrifice of Jesus would bring you close to Himself. He was thinking about how He would make you complete in Him. You are worth it all.

Receive His love. Let it pour into every place in your heart. Let it wash over every negative thought, let it destroy every stronghold in your mind, and heal every heartache. Let His love flood every fiber of your being, causing warm peace and joy to enter in. You are worth it.

Speak this from your heart today: *"I am worth it. I am special to God. I am so loved by Him. No matter the mistakes I've made, I am forgiven and washed from all unrighteousness by the blood of Jesus. I receive His love, His mercy and His righteousness. Thank You Lord for rescuing me and loving me. I surrender to You."*

(Read Romans 5:1; Romans 3:24-26; Ephesians 2:13; Hebrews 9:14, Hebrews 9:22; 1John 1:7; Romans 5:10; Romans 8:1; Romans 8:30; John 5:24; 1Thessalonians 1:10)

Courageous Faith

"Be strong and courageous, for you are the one who will lead these people to possess all the land I swore to their ancestors I would give them"
Joshua 1:6, NLT

♛

Settle this in your heart today: "I am who God says I am. I have what God says I have. I can do what God says I can do, and I will be what God says I will be. There's nothing too hard for me, because there's nothing too hard for God!"

Maybe God has asked you to do something you've never done before. You are in uncharted waters and you may have no point of reference and not one example in your life to model after. Yet, God chose you, and He wants you to have courageous faith. Here's how you can...

Write it down.

Create a vision board, a drawing, or write down the task God gave you. The vision you pen will be what fuels you. (see Habakkuk 2:2,3)

Feed your faith.

The more you hear God's word and act on it, the more your faith will grow like a giant. Record yourself speaking God's word and listen to it over and over again. (see Romans 10:17)

Surround yourself with people who believe in you.

Everyone isn't going to champion your cause and support your bold steps toward obeying God. Instead of allowing their discouragement to deter you, surround yourself with people who believe in you and who are full of faith.

Say what you believe.

The Apostle Paul said, "I believed, therefore, I spoke" (see 2 Corinthians 4:13) When it comes to having courageous faith, you will have to declare it openly, especially in the face of those who doubt you and your God.

Prayer: *Father God, I thank You for Your work in my heart and in my life. You are wonderful! Thank You for nourishing my faith and helping me to believe in You and in myself. I often feel scared, but don't let that stop me from obeying You. I love You. Thank You for giving me courageous faith. In Jesus name, Amen.*

A Prayer Partner

"Again I say to you, that if two of you agree on earth about anything that they may ask, it shall be done for them by My Father who is in heaven. For where two or three have gathered together in My name, I am there in their midst."
Matthew 18:19-20

⚜

I met my prayer partner my freshmen year in college. We lived in the same dormitory, and I knew from the start that God wanted us to connect. So I befriended her and discovered she loved to pray just like me.

Over the 17 years we have been friends, we have prayed through losses, through sickness, through weariness, through financial needs, family issues, and believed God for great things. I believe our prayers are why God brought us together—the friendship is extra. Every time we come together or talk on the phone, by the end of it, we are praying. What a blessing!

The Bible says, every good and perfect gift comes from above (see James 1:17). You are not alone, left to stand and fight alone. God will bless you with that sister that loves you enough to stand with you in prayer. Maybe it's a co-worker, a next door neighbor, a colleague, or a sister at church, ask God to give you someone that loves God, loves you and loves to pray.

Hence, we have the key qualities of a prayer partner:

She loves God.

If she loves God, she will care more about pleasing Him than pleasing you. This is powerful in a prayer partner because out of her love for God, she will help keep your focus on Him.

She loves you.

A prayer partner cares about everything you're going through, and when you pray together, you can sense her love and heart's desire for God's perfect will to be accomplished within you and through you.

She loves to pray.

She loves spending time in God's presence. She knows where healing takes place, where empty cups are filled and where God does His greatest works in our hearts. She understands the significance of prayer.

Prayer: *Father, I desire a prayer partner. Send me that person that can stand with me in prayer and I stand with her. I pray she loves You, loves me, and will love to pray. Thank You my Father God. In Jesus' name, Amen.*

(Read Acts 4:24-31; Revelation 11:4)

Your best life is in front of you.

"Brothers, I do not consider myself to have taken hold of it. But one thing indeed: Forgetting the things behind and reaching forward to the things ahead" Philippians 3:13, Berean Literal Bible.

I'm just going to say it...You're not hurting anyone but yourself when you give in to the enemy because of what someone did to you. I'm sorry they hurt you. I'm sorry they didn't believe in you. I'm sorry they weren't there when you needed them most. It hurts, I know it does. But you know what, my friend? You can either use this as fuel or as an excuse. The greatest revenge is to go full force into the things of God, to go full force into your purpose, to give God your broken heart and let Him kiss it and make it better. God can give you more new memories that will take the place of all the old hurtful ones.

He can show you that there is life after heartbreak. There is more life to live. Your best life is in front of you, not behind you. Reeeaaacchh forward. Reeeaaacchh forward. Reeeaaacchh forward into God's perfect plan. You can do it. You will find grace waiting in front of you. You will find happiness waiting in front you. You will find healing...waiting... in front of you.

Prayer: *Lord, I pray for my sister reading this now. You know exactly what she is feeling. Help her Lord to see the same thing You showed me when I was hurting beyond belief. You showed me the same love that I encountered the first day I surrendered to you. Show her that Powerful, Everlasting, Unconditional, Never Changing Love. Dissolve her fears. Heal her pain. Hug her heart. Remove all hopelessness, and help her Reeeaaacchh forward. In Jesus name, Amen.*

Share Your Story

"Has the Lord redeemed you? Then speak out! Tell others he has redeemed you from your enemies"
Psalm 107:2, NLT.

♔

The first time I shared my testimony was in a formal setting, and involved a great deal of planning and preparation. I stood at a podium in front of a group of people, in a church, and I talked for about 20 -30 minutes on how God has transformed me from a broken, beaten, bruised alcoholic, to a beautiful, bold, blessed daughter of the King. While it was a powerful experience, it took a great deal of time and energy, and I wondered how people did this all the time. I was a pretty new Christian at the time, so giving testimony was a brand new experience for me. I thought the only way to share it was in a formal setting such as this.

What I didn't realize at the time is that I am giving testimony to God's amazing love every single day. Every time I share a story of what God has done in my life or in the lives of others I know, I am giving testimony. Every time I speak out that I am a recovering alcoholic by God's grace - I am giving testimony. When I live my faith out by serving others and showing God's love to others - I am giving testimony. When people see me reading the Bible in public, or stating that I am a Christian - I am giving testimony!

A Facebook post, an offer to pray for someone, a sharing of a quick story, or even a simple "God bless you" to someone, can be a way of giving testimony to our amazing God. How will you testify today?

Prayer: *God, you deserve all the praise and glory for the wonderful things you do in our lives! Please give us a new boldness to speak out about your wonderful deeds to others. Please don't let us shy away from every opportunity that comes our way to give testimony to Your amazing grace and love! In Jesus' name, Amen*

Be deeply encouraged.

"No unbelief made him waver concerning the promise of God, but he grew strong in his faith as he gave glory to God, fully convinced that God was able to do what he had promised"
Romans 4:20-21, ESV.

ቍ

I don't know the power of God's love and mercy until I make a complete mess of things. I don't know the power God's light until I walk through the darkest valley of my life. I don't know Him to be a true friend until someone I love leaves me. I don't fully realize He lives in me until I am pressed unimaginably. It is my daily sufferings that give me hope. It is my experiences that cause my faith to grow.

It is not our light that makes us beautiful, it is our struggle, and our determination to not let our light die.

The Bible says, "...we rejoice in our sufferings, knowing that suffering produces endurance, and endurance produces character, and character produces hope, and hope does not put us to shame, because God's love has been poured into our hearts through the Holy Spirit who has been given to us" (see Romans 5:3-5).

What you are going through right now may not feel good and it may not look good, but my sister know that it's working for your good. Let it grow you and deepen your faith. God will reveal that is He is your God and He is on your side! It's not over for you.

Be deeply encouraged and filled with hope! God will be glorified in your life!

Prayer: *Father, I thank You for Your promise to me. It's an honor to know You and an honor to be called by You. Thank You for being with me through every trial. Continue to grow my faith in you Lord and help me to trust You more. Be glorified in my life. In Jesus name, Amen.*

(Read Philippians 3:8-10)

Faith to Faith

*"For therein is the righteousness of God revealed
from faith to faith: as it is written, The just shall
live by faith"* Romans 1:17.

꩜

You can trust God! If He came through
before, He will come through again and
again. He will continue to demonstrate His
love for you over and over again until you
understand just how much He loves you and
has your back. He is good!

Fear sees obstacles, while faith sees
opportunities. Fear causes us to doubt and
complain, while faith causes us to rejoice
and praise God. A characteristic of faith is
thankfulness. A thankful heart rejoices over
what God has already done and what He's
about to do. Let thankfulness carry you
through into the next demonstration of
God's faithfulness in your life.

Settle in your heart that you will live
from faith to faith!

81

Prayer: *Father God, thank You for demonstrating Your love for me. Forgive me for every time I've doubted You. You are trustworthy and You are faithful! I'm thankful I know You and I praise You for what You have already done in my life. I'm excited about Your divine plans and purpose. Help me to settle it in my heart to live from faith to faith. In Jesus' Name, Amen.*

Don't change.

*"For we are his workmanship, created in Christ
Jesus for good works, which God prepared
beforehand, that we should walk in them"*
Ephesians 2:10, ESV.

The world will try to make you feel like something is wrong with you. They will say that you are too loving, too kind, too giving, that your heart is too big, or you're too this or that. No, don't believe the world. Keep being who you are. Keep being the great blessing you are. Keep being like Jesus and drawing men to the Lord with the love He has placed within you.

You've been changed for a reason. You've been purified for a divine purpose. Even when you experience sin in your personal life, don't let that change you. At your core, you are God's beautiful design, you are His workmanship, created in Christ Jesus. You are a special gift from God.

The work God has accomplished in you is not something you can reverse or stop being. I know sometimes you wish you didn't love as hard as you do, you wish you didn't have such a great big heart, but that's who you are. God's wisdom will guide you, but you keep being who He made you to be. This world needs you just the way you are.

Don't change.

Prayer: *Father God, I love You. Thank You for encouraging me deeply in my soul. Thank You for Your work in me, your work through me, and Your work around me. Help me not to change for anyone, but be who You made me to be. Be glorified in me, and I mean that sincerely. In Jesus' name, Amen.*

You have some declaring to do!

"I shall not die, but live, and declare the works of the LORD" Psalms 118:17, KJV.

When you could be dead, but God caused you to live, you have some declaring to do. When it's a miracle that you are here, you have some declaring to do. When you wanted to backslide, but God kept you from going back, you have some declaring to do. There has been a supernatural work in you, and now there must be a supernatural work through you. Your declaring the works of the Lord will cause all around you to know and recognize the power of your God.

To declare in this verse means to inscribe, to recount, and to celebrate. Don't hold back your declaration of what the Lord has done in your life. Write about it, talk about it, shout about it, and testify to the goodness of your great God! Don't allow anyone to make you feel as though what He brought you through is too shameful to mention out loud. The only shame is in keeping quiet. If God brought you through it, He wants you to greatly rejoice about it and shout it on the mountain top! The only time we have God's permission to be rooftop women is when we are boldly declaring what God has said and what He has done (see Matthew 10:27)!

We overcome by the blood of the Lamb and by the word of our testimony (see Revelation 12:11).

Prayer: *Father God, thank You for Your mighty work in me, Your work through me and Your work around me. Help me not be afraid to open up and declare to others what You have done in my life. I pray my testimony touches someone and helps them come to know You for themselves. In Jesus' Name, Amen.*

The Power of Release

"Casting all your care upon Him, for He cares for you" 1 Peter 5:7.

꒰꒱

When you are set on fulfilling God's purpose for your life, you must remember to release people and situations to God. Why? Because it will destroy you and will hinder your spiritual progress if you don't. Obey God and release them. You can't free them by your power. You can't deliver anyone in your own strength. You can't change anything about that situation by yourself. You can't, but God can. And if anything miraculous is going to happen, it's going to be by the power of God's Holy Spirit.

Don't take upon yourself a responsibility God didn't give you. Don't worry yourself trying to figure out what you can do to save them. Do only what God tells you to do and then release it to Him. I know it's tough, but you must know that God cares for that person AND for you. Stand back and watch Him work.

God is saying by His Spirit, "I will do what I promised. Trust Me. Entrust them to Me. I can go where you can't. I can see where You can't. Nothing is hidden from Me. Release them to Me. Give it all to Me and You will see Me demonstrate My love and My power in ways You thought were impossible."

A Challenge for You: Make a list of every person you are carrying on your heart and mind. Go down the list and say, "Lord, I release ___(say their name)___ to You. I entrust them to Your care. Have Your way in their lives. In Jesus name."

Prayer: *Father God, I care so much for the people in my life, and I want to see them experience the life and freedom that I am experiencing in You. I exercise the power You have given me through Jesus and I release them by faith into Your care. I trust You. In Jesus' name, Amen.*

Raw Forgiveness

*"For if you forgive other people when they sin
against you, your heavenly Father will
also forgive you"* Matthew 6:14, NIV.

For most people when we hear the words
"forgive them" our skin begins to crawl. It
has to be *the* most difficult thing to do when
you have been hurt and emotionally scarred.
And I'm not talking about forgiving them
with empty words, I'm talking about
forgiving them wholeheartedly to the point
where you are compelled to earnestly pray
for them frequently. It's all the more
difficult to do when you have to face them
often.

But the Lord has commanded us to
follow His footsteps in everything, including
forgiveness. We must forgive others just as
He has forgiven us. Now a days people
forgive certain things but not all. It's like we
have a "severity of offense" checklist and we

go by that list in order to forgive like Jesus did. We are so wrong, my friends. The moment God forgave us, He didn't go by any checklist, He entirely forgave us because without His forgiveness we wouldn't have access to our eternal salvation.

The opening scripture tells us to forgive in order to be forgiven. Although this can be a hard truth to receive, it's ultimately for our own good. How? Because forgiving them, detoxifies you!

Forgiving others is about you, not them, so it's in our best interest to live a toxic free life. We will always encounter betrayals and offense, but we must forgive right away and refuse to allow the toxins of unforgiveness to pile up. However, if we refuse to wholeheartedly forgive right away, we will be like an atomic bomb waiting to explode. Unfortunately, we end up hurting innocent people. Let's be wise and obedient. Let's forgive and be set free.

Prayer: *Father God, I can't count the times You've forgiven me. So I freely give what You've given me. I release any unforgiveness that has been stored up in my heart for _____(fill in the blank)_____. I forgive them right now by faith. I ask that You bless them and cause them to see Your love for them. I also pray that heal my heart, heal my emotions and fill me with Your love. In Jesus name, Amen!*

(Read Matthew 18:21-25; Proverbs 21:13; Mark 11:25-26; Ephesians 4:32)

No More Stinking Thinking

"Finally, brothers and sisters, whatever is true, whatever is noble, whatever is right, whatever is pure, whatever is lovely, whatever is admirable--if anything is excellent or praiseworthy--think about such things" Philippians 4:8, NIV.

Some people have a drinking problem, or a smoking problem. Some have an eating problem. Some have a porn problem. Me? I have a thinking problem. I can resist the temptation to go and purchase and consume liquor. I can ignore a popup ad on the internet to watch porn. But when the enemy presents a negative toxic thought to my mind, I have to on purpose say, "No, I'm not thinking on that! I cast that imagination down in Jesus name and bring that thought captive in the obedience of Christ (see 2 Corinthians 10:5)." If I don't, my mind gets all burdened down and preoccupied with the wrong stuff. The only solution is to change my thinking.

God teaches us that we can train our minds to think on the right things. In Philippians 4:8, we find all of the good stuff we are to fill our minds with: thoughts that are true, noble and right, pure, lovely, of good report. Then He says, if there is any virtue and if there is any praise, think on these things. That sounds easy, but for an introvert like me, with an active mind and a vivid imagination, it takes plenty of effort.

However, with God's help and our willing hearts, we can train our minds to believe the best rather than assume the worst. We can think on positive things rather than negative things. We can let peace guard our hearts and minds through Jesus. We can choose to spend quality time in prayer, praise and meditating on God's promises, which is the breeding ground for a disciplined and well-trained mind.

Prayer: *Father God, You are my God and I love*

You. I need Your help with my stinking thinking. Renew my mind Lord and help me to fill it with right things that glorify You. I submit to You and I receive Your wisdom and Your grace to walk this out in my daily life. In Jesus' name, Amen.

Indicators of Greatness

"...but the people that do know their God shall be strong, and do exploits" Daniel 11:32, KJV.

Great Activity
The enemy wouldn't be fighting you so hard if you didn't have something of great value inside of you. Even in this, know that it is not the activity of the enemy that indicates greatness, but the activity of God in your heart and life. Let Him continue His work in you.

Great Passion
When the fire within you is greater than the fire that surrounds you, you are headed towards great things for God's glory.

Great Obedience
You are headed towards greatness when you can't rest until you do what God is prompting you to do, even the smallest

command. Know that there's a special grace to do what He said, right at the moment when He said it.

Great Love

Your desire to please God must be greater than your desire to be hurt and angry.

Great Boldness

Even though you feel scared, choose to do it anyway—shaking and all. Don't wait to feel brave. Obey God and bravery will come. You will grow more fearless with every victory.

Great Solutions

Don't sit around complaining about the problem; be solution-oriented. Spend 10% of your conversation talking about the problem, and 90% of time discussing the solution.

Great Perseverance

With every challenge, become stronger. What the enemy meant for your bad, God will turn it around for your good.

Great Light

Let Him flood every dark and hidden place in your heart with His truth. Desire to receive His truth in your inward parts and He will cause you to be a great light in a grossly dark world.

Great Help

God will take you from being Forsaken to being Sought After. Because He has given you an assignment that's too big for you to do alone, He will bring people to help you do the great work He's given you.

Prayer: *Father God, thank You for speaking directly to my heart. You are great and You are faithful. Have Your way in me and be glorified in my life. I receive all that You have waiting for me. In Jesus name, Amen.*

Lost and Found

Jesus answered, "I am the way and the truth and the life. No one comes to the Father except through me"
John 14:6, NIV.

Scared and alone,
hiding, trying not to be found,
looking searching, lost from the flock
so the lamb had thought.
Broken, weeping, her Shepard waiting,
Watching, knowing she will return.
In her ear she hears his whisper,
"Lamb of mine, come on home,
you will be safe, I am the way,
the truth and the life, don't
be afraid, let me guide the way"
Home at last, growing strong in her Father's arms,
leaving fear behind, made more aware.
Thankful for his grace,
thankful for her sins washed away.
Glory to his name,
to he who is love that leads the way.

I wrote this in the beginning of my journey. It came to me as a song and was a great comfort from our Heavenly Father in a time of the unknown. I was scared and I was lost, but our Father found me and He is guiding me. Don't be afraid, our King is the way! If you have been away from Him, He is waiting to welcome you back home.

Prayer: *Father I thank you for finding me, I have been away but I am home. I choose you and the way you have planned and purposed for me. Forgive me Jesus for not trusting you. Forgive me for being afraid. I know now that you are the way, the truth and the life and you are the gift of grace given to me to enter the kingdom gates to our Father. I love you. In Jesus' name, Amen.*

Encourage Yourself

"Let no foul or polluting language, nor evil word nor unwholesome or worthless talk [ever] come out of your mouth, but only such [speech] as is good and beneficial to the spiritual progress of others, as is fitting to the need and the occasion, that it may be a blessing and give grace (God's favor) to those who hear it."

Ephesians 4:29, Amplified

Have you ever called yourself "stupid", "slow", "crazy", or any other destructive words? Surely those words didn't make you feel any better about yourself. Many of us understand that we aren't to destroy others with our words, but we must not destroy ourselves either. Speak these words over yourself: I am a treasure! I will make it! I am God's masterpiece! I am more than an overcomer through Jesus! I am God's daughter! He has a plan for my life and a bright future! I am so loved by God! I am fearfully and wonderfully made!

Words like these minister life to your soul. When everyone is telling you what you can't do and who you are not, stand and speak out of your mouth that you can and you will. Begin to encourage yourself in the Lord. Prophesy to yourself. Comfort your heart with your own words. Minister life to yourself, and you will find that the same words you use to build up yourself will be the very same words you minister to those around you.

Prayer: *Father, thank you for encouraging me. No matter what others think or say, I say what You say. I am Your daughter and You are my Father. As you build me up, help me to build up others. In Jesus' name, Amen.*

Know Who You Are

"But by the grace of God I am what I am: and his grace which was bestowed upon me was not in vain; but I laboured more abundantly than they all: yet not I, but the grace of God which was with me."
1 Corinthians 15:10

♔

You are not your past. You are not your failures. You are not your state. You are a daughter of the King. You already know who God is, now be reminded today of who you are in Him:

I am smart. I am important. I am a world changer. I am brave and courageous. I am fearfully and wonderfully made. I am beautiful. I am called by God to do great things. I am strong. I melt in His presence, yet stand strong in the face of adversity. I can't stop running because Jesus didn't stop for me. I am a finisher. I am the right woman for the job. I am a winner. I am so loved. I am richly blessed. I am rooted and grounded. I am abundantly graced. I am my brother and sister's keeper. I am empowered to lead. I am an overcomer. I am more than a conqueror. Greater is He that is in me than he that's in the world. I am a daughter of the King no matter how I feel. No matter how it looks I will see His promises manifested in my life. I am patient and kind. I am truthful. I am hidden in Christ. I am an end time soldier in His army. I was born for such a time as this. I have what it takes. I am resourceful. I am wise. I wear God's grace beautifully. I am who God says I am and I will do what He says I will do.

Prayer: Father, help me stay reminded of who I am in You. Help me not to let my problems define me. You define me, Lord. You are my God and I belong to You. In Jesus Name, Amen.

He is Preparing You

"But let patience have her perfect work, that ye may be perfect and entire, wanting nothing."
James 1:7, KJV

༒

Where is God's man for me? Where's my Boaz, my Mr. Right and my knight in shining armor? When we are waiting for our future spouse, it can seem as though it's taking an eternity. We've already made plans and the delay is messing up our plans, because in our minds, we were supposed to be married by now.

So how does God respond? He says the same thing He's been telling us since the beginning of time. "Rest in Me and wait patiently for Me (see Psalm 37:7)." God is preparing you and him. While you may think He is moving too slow, let Him finish preparing you, healing you, instructing you, growing you and refining you. He will present you to your husband in His perfect timing. Marriage is no play thing. It is serious business that you have to be physically, mentally, emotionally, and spiritually equipped to handle.

The job of a man isn't to fill a void in your life or complete you. You are complete in God. He satisfies you. He enriches you and makes you feel good about you. Impatience can cause us to fall for the imitation that often comes before the real thing. You don't want someone that looks good and sounds good, but yet something just isn't right. The best candidate for your heart is someone with a different spirit like Joshua. Someone with a heart for God like David. Someone that will fit you like a hand in glove, who will be your bestfriend and your greatest source of support and encouragement in good times and bad. Someone you can be yourself around and who pushes you to be all that God called to be. God can give you someone that will love Him more than he loves you and someone who will love you more than he loves himself.

Don't settle. No matter what your past have been and no matter how many children you may have, you deserve a good Godly man. If Jesus saw you as worth dying for, God has a man that will see you as worth marrying and worth caring for. Receive His word today, "Rest in Me and wait patiently for Me."

Prayer: *Thank you Father God for encouraging me. You love me and only want the best for me. I believe I am ready to be a wife to the man You have for me, but help me wait on Your perfect timing. Prepare me for that blessed man and help me recognize when You bring him into my life. In Jesus' name, Amen.*

(Read: Colossians 2:10; 1 Peter 3:3-4; 1 Corinthians 2:9-10; 1 Corinthians 7:34)

A message from God's heart for you.

"You will see My mighty fist and My strong muscle displayed in your life like never before. You have wanted to see My glory. From your spirit you cried, "Lord show me Your glory." So My glory you will see. You have waited and now the vision speaks. Now My dream for you will come to pass. The place I have brought you to, no one will be able to separate you from it. The place My love has brought you to, no one can rob you of it. And what my love has taught you, no one can cause you to unlearn it. It's yours. Rejoice in the land of the living! Rejoice in My deliverance and in My special care of you. Rejoice that you know and understand My love, My character and My nature to bless those who diligently seek Me. This is a time of seeing what I have longed for you to see, tasting what I have longed for you to taste, and receiving what I have longed to give you. It is time of great and tremendous rejoicing on your part and great action and power on Mine." Says the Spirit of the Lord.

(Read Psalms 63:2; Psalms 27:13; 2 Timothy 3:14)

Let God Plant You

"To all who mourn in Israel, he will give a crown of beauty for ashes, a joyous blessing instead of mourning, festive praise instead of despair. In their righteousness, they will be like great oaks that the LORD has planted for his own glory"
Isaiah 61:3, NLT.

A seed doesn't just need water in order to grow; it needs the right amount of everything. It needs the right amount of water, soil, sunlight, and love. A seed doesn't get to choose its own soil, the gardener does.

When it comes to church membership, every believer must be planted somewhere in order to grow and blossom. However, you don't get to choose where you are planted, God does. He chooses the right environment that is perfect for you and your family. You don't just need good preaching or a great kids program. You need an environment that's perfect for your optimum growth and spiritual development.

God is the Gardener and where He plants you, you will prosper. Where He plants you, you will be challenged. Where He plants you, you will grow and spread your wings to soar. That place will bring out the best in you and you will in turn give your best back to it.

Are you growing? Are you blossoming? Are you soaring? Are you being challenged? Is your life producing visible results? If not, you must ask yourself if whether you have been planted by God or if you have chosen your own soil. When you plant yourself, you develop weeds and your life doesn't produce much. Pray for God to plant you and you will begin to grow and blossom for the glory of God.

Prayer: *Father, I pray You direct me to the church that is the right environment for me and my family. I want to give my all in serving your people and learn more about You. Lead me and guide me to where You want me to be planted. In Jesus' Name, Amen.*

More of My Spirit

"But the Helper (Comforter, Advocate, Intercessor-Counselor, Strengthener, Standby), the Holy Spirit, whom the Father will send in My name [in My place, to represent Me and act on My behalf], He will teach you all things. And He will help you remember everything that I have told you."
John 14:26, Amplified

Precious Holy Spirit
My heavenly guide
I welcome you now
Stand by my side
I come to you empty
Fill me completely
My soul needs refreshing
and I am yielded

There are many gifts you can receive in this world, but nothing compares to the precious gift of the Holy Spirit. Jesus promised to send Him and He kept His promise. He is our Comforter, Counselor, Intercessor, Advocate, Strengthener and Standby. When we rest in Him, He moves.

You have been looking for a breakthrough, you have been wondering when your time will come, and when things will finally happen for you. You have been battered by the storms of life and the winds just won't let up. You haven't felt the warmth of God's presence in a long time and you have grown despondent. But our Father God is saying to you right now...

"My Spirit is with you. My Spirit is here to fill you completely. Welcome my Holy Spirit into your life and in your heart. Yield to Him. He will comfort you. He will counsel you. He is interceding for you. He will advocate for you. He will strengthen you, and will stand by you always. He will never leave Your side. He is your refreshing. He is your constant reminder of Who I am and what I have promised you. He is what you've truly been longing for. More of My Spirit, I say. More of My Spirit is waiting for you. Receive more of My Spirit."

Challenge and Responsibility

"The Lord God is my strength [my source of courage, my invincible army]; He has made my feet [steady and sure] like hinds' feet and makes me walk [forward with spiritual confidence] on my high places [of challenge and responsibility]."
Habakkuk 3:19, Amplified

Don't be moved. No matter how you feel, you are a world changer. You are living in the greatest time in human history, and just when it appears like the devil is winning, God's grace is abounding. He is moving with great force like a mighty undercurrent. He is sweeping across the world uniting His people, bringing revival and causing His sons and daughters to be revealed.

Keep advancing God's Kingdom. Keep walking in love and humility. Keep persevering by faith. Stay hungry for more of Him. Keep resting in His love. This is a great time to be alive and we have no time to waste. Go into your place of prayer and let God fill you with Himself. Make your relationship with God your top priority. It is the most important relationship in your life.

Prayer: *(deep breath) My Father, my God. I receive your words, I receive your fresh wind and I receive your love. You are moving by your Spirit. Help me move with you. I don't want to be left behind. Set me on fire for you and renew my thirst and hunger for you. Grace me Lord for these days and help to lead a lost and dying world to your Love. In Jesus' name, Amen.*

A Divine Purpose

"A man's gift makes room for him, and brings him before great men" Proverbs 18:16, NKJV.

In Bible history, we learn of Esther, a Jewess maiden who was chosen by king Ahasuerus to be his wife. To the king, she was by far the most beautiful woman in all the land of Persia. In her new position as queen, God was able to use her to save thousands of Jews from being killed. There was a divine purpose for her beauty and a divine purpose for her promotion as queen.

Likewise, there is a divine purpose for your design, your personality, looks, gifts, talents, and skill set. And when God causes any of these things to bring you success and promotion, remember that it's for a divine purpose to bless someone.

In the words of a dear mother in the Lord...

"Yes those gifts are limitless and amazing! The manifested sons of God are raising up, and by the Holy Spirit are bringing great revelation for the season and seasons yet to come. Sound the alarm and stay position in Christ. We are mandated to keep our eyes fixed on Him alone. His Kingdom is here and it is advancing into every arena. Lifestyles are being converted as we yield and submit to the Truth Giver who ever lives to bring the transformation with our living by and in our new nature." - Barbara Joanne Bell-Claxton

Prayer: *Lord, I offer to You every gift and talent You have given me. I ask that as You cause these gifts to bring promotion. Help me to remember my kingdom assignment and stay in position for maximum effectiveness. In Jesus' name, Amen.*

A Strong Woman

"But by the grace of God I am what I am: and his grace which was bestowed upon me was not in vain; but I laboured more abundantly than they all: yet not I, but the grace of God which was with me."
1 Corinthians 15:10

I come from a family where the women are strong, industrious and independent. They are assertive and speak their mind freely. They know what they want and work hard to obtain it. They handle whatever life throws at them and can bounce back from the most terrible situations.

For years I've wanted to make the women in my family proud by following their example of strength, but I soon realized that God made me different. I'm not always so sure of myself, don't always say what I feel, and the slightest amount of opposition and pressure can turn me into a ball of tears. In relationships, I'm quick to express my deepest fears and doubts no matter how confident I appear to be.

In this, God has redefined strength for me. I believe strength is humility. It is knowing what you can't do, and letting God do it through you. Strength is knowing your gifting and letting God anoint even the things you're great at. Strength is total dependence on God and on the connection you have to your brothers and sisters in Christ. It is expressing your fears with no shame of opinions changing about you. It is the determination to not let your light die because you know who you are in Christ and Who He is in you.

Prayer: *Father God, I ask that you renew my mind and show me Your definition of strength. Remove every stronghold in my mind and every unfair expectation I've placed on myself. I receive Your love and Your mercy. Bless me Lord with Your peace and strengthen me to be the woman You've called me to be. In Jesus name, Amen.*

Move out of the way and let God do it!

"But thou, O LORD, art a shield for me; my glory, and the lifter up of mine head." Psalm 3:3

♔

One of the hardest things to do is to step aside and let God handle a situation. You may have been wronged, falsely accused, and mistreated, but as angry as you may feel you have to use wisdom in how you handle it. Place your trust in God and receive His wisdom. He will guide you and instruct you. And if He says, "do nothing", do nothing. Your nothing gives Him room to do something about it. He is King and He is in control.

Trust that God will vindicate you. Trust that He will clear your name. Trust that He will prepare a table before you right in the presence of your enemies. Trust that He will turn the heart of the king because the king's heart is in His hands. Move out of the way and let Him be what you need Him to be. The consequences of taking matters into your own hands are endless, but the rewards of letting God fight your battles are great! Move out of the way and let God do it!

Prayer: *Yes Lord! I receive Your word. You are my God and I am Yours. Help me to step aside and let You into this situation. Help me leave it alone and trust You. You knew these things would happen way before I did. Vindicate me Lord. Be my defense. I lift You up and I put my trust in You. I receive Your peace now. In Jesus' Name, Amen.*

(Read Proverbs 21:1)

Kept

"Who keeps us in life And does not allow our feet to slip." Psalm 66:9, NIV

Can you just stop for a brief moment in the midst of your busy day and think about how in the world you've made it this far? How is it that you made it alive from all of those horrible situations? I know we can all relate this morning that life has been anything but easy. We can all agree that God's goodness and His protection has always KEPT us. That no matter how difficult the situation may have been or how distant He's felt, He has never left your side, He's KEPT you.

Those moments when you thought you were going to lose your mind, God KEPT you sane. Those moments when you thought you couldn't go forward any longer, God KEPT you moving. Those moments when you wanted to lash out to those people that have wronged you, God KEPT your mouth shut. Those moments when you barely had any money to eat, God KEPT your stomach full, He KEPT your lights on and your rent paid. When you faced situations that made you weak in the knees, He's KEPT you standing.

I can go on and on but I know you can clearly see how He's KEPT His promises over your life. So today, KEEP your first love for Him burning and start thanking Him for what He has done and for what He will continue doing in your life. He is faithful yesterday, today and forever more. He has KEPT you woman of God, so rejoice and love on Him. Shout out, "I AM A KEPT WOMAN"!

Prayer: *Thank You King Jesus for keeping me together throughout all of life's circumstances. As I reflect on this today, I just want to tell you thank You. Continue keeping me in the palm of Your hand, in Jesus name, Amen!*

Hug, apologize and say, "*I love you*".

"This is my commandment, that ye love one another, as I have loved you" John 15:12.

⚜

I grew up with a sister, and even though we would argue all of the time, we quickly made up because my mother didn't tolerate strife in her house. If we fought, she would make us hug, apologize and say, "I love you". Then we were back to playing again. This is what true sisterhood looked like to me. It was ingrained in my mind that sisters always love and forgave each other no matter what. So when I became older and God blessed me with sisters in Christ, I just knew that if anything went down, if there was any drama, any disagreements or any strife, we would hug, apologize, say "I love you" and go back to playing again.

The sad reality is that many women

don't know this kind of love among sisters in the Lord.

As sisters, we live in God's house, He is our heavenly Father, and we abide by His rules. If my mother didn't tolerate strife and division in her house, surely God doesn't either. He commands that we love one another as He have loved us. He doesn't suggest it or say to only love if we feel like it. He commands it.

Our sisterly bond in Christ must deepen and be strengthened so that the world can know that we're truly His disciples by how we love each other.

Prayer: *Yes Lord. Thank You for speaking to my heart. Forgive me for not loving my sisters like I should. I ask that You show me how to love the way You have loved me. I want to do whatever makes You happy. So help me God to look past faults and see my sister's heart. I pray You bring a spirit of love and unity among Your daughters. We need You Lord. Help us learn to love each other in a way that glorifies You. In Jesus' name, Amen.*

Believe

"For assuredly, I say to you, whoever says to this mountain, 'Be removed and be cast into the sea,' and does not doubt in his heart, but believes that those things he says will be done, he will have whatever he says" Mark 11:23, NKJV.

Believe when all of the odds are against you. Believe when the world isn't for you. These words are simple, but true. When you believe, Jesus breathes the breath of life inside of you. Believe when the mountains that you face are too big through your eyes. Believe when they say you will never amount to anything. Believe when your family and friends turn against you. Believe when they say, "It won't be long before she falls again." Believe in Jesus when they tell you that you are crazy. Believe when all you can see are dark clouds. Believe when there seems to be no way out. Believe even when people say, "You are worthless." Believe in

Jesus when they tell you that you will always be in addiction. Believe when your children have been taken from you due to your poor choices. Believe in Jesus when you have lost your way. Believe when you think you can't go on one more day. Believe when you have lost everything time and time again. Believe when you are discouraged. Believe when you are facing a struggle that holds no view. Believe in that something inside of you. For God sent His Son Jesus. Jesus believed enough to die for us. For He who sent us makes no mistakes. His Spirit within us gives us the faith.

There is nothing we can't accomplish through Jesus Christ, from the earliest dawn to the darkest of nights. He has a way of breaking through the darkness. He did it for me, and He will do it for you. Jesus is our Helper. He is our Friend. He is our Healer and Deliverer til the very end. Call on Him, He will always be there, to lift you up and show you He cares. He makes your crooked paths straight and puts hope in your heart. He is our Blessed Assurance and has been from the start. Remember the One who has always held your hand. Believe in His purpose and His unfailing plan.

Prayer: *Father, lately I have focused more on my circumstances rather than You. I have called on my ability to do things instead of Yours. Today I choose to believe in all that You have for me no matter what. I love You and am so grateful for Your faithfulness. Thanks for always believing in me. In Jesus name I pray. Amen*

(Mark 9:23; John 20:27; Genesis 15:6)

See Through Lens of Grace

"There is therefore now no condemnation to them which are in Christ Jesus, who walk not after the flesh, but after the spirit" Romans 8:1.

Take a moment and think about what this Scripture means to you.

When we come into a true knowledge of Jesus, we will always look at our lives and see where we and others have fallen short. We can't see God's love and mercy because all we see is our sin. It is the tree that blocks our view. But if we look at our lives and see Jesus, how He has redeemed, and delivered us, there is no sin blocking us anymore. We then can see Him and receive from Him.

See your life through the lens of grace, not through the lens of condemnation. Fix your eyes on the truth of God's word and He will change your heart and mind. You are redeemed through Jesus! You are loved because of Jesus! You are made holy and put in right standing with God through Jesus! Your sins can't disqualify you and your good works can't qualify you! Everything you are and everything you have is because of Jesus. Tell condemnation goodbye, and say hello to a life of grace and favor with God.

Prayer: *Father God, I thank you that there is therefore now no condemnation to me. I'm in Christ Jesus. I walk not after the flesh, but after the spirit. You're not condemning me, so I will not condemn myself. I receive the lens of grace. I can see Jesus and I can see how blessed I truly am in Jesus' name, Amen.*

Loneliness vs. Solitude

no one likes loneliness
it sounds like what it is
none are happy there
none are happy where
no friend comes
but solitude
beautiful solitude
it's a place
of sweet solace
you go there by choice
to hear yourself think
enjoy your own thoughts
and appreciate who you are
visit there often friend
live there even when
in a crowded room
your place
of solitude

"Cure my loneliness Lord or I'm moving back home." I told God one day in prayer.

Amazing how I thought I could actually give Him an ultimatum. The loneliness I felt seemed unbearable. I was missing my friends terribly while living in a new city.

While some are scared of bats, some are terrified of snakes, or maybe heights, my deepest fear was being left alone. Having to go alone. Endure trials alone. And so it goes with living by faith, you are challenged to face every one of your fears. Whatever you fear you can't do, God will show you that you can. I wanted friendship, so He gave me a season of solitude. He gave me something no one can ever take away from me—a friendship with myself.

Friends come and go, but you will always have you—every second and every minute. You have yourself through every trial and every triumph. And since you are with yourself all of the time, you might as well learn how to enjoy your company. In solitude you learn to accept yourself as God does, forgive yourself, challenge yourself, love yourself and comfort yourself. You learn how to encourage yourself when you're down. How to tell yourself to get up and try again. How to be honest with yourself. How to keep yourself humble when you are on top. You learn all of the qualities of being a good friend. The greatest friend to others is the one that's the greatest friend to themselves. And until someone can treat you better than you treat your solitude, they don't deserve you.

When God brings you into a season of solitude, He has a plan to enrich you so that you can enrich others. He does an amazing work inside you to prepare you for the great work He will do outside of you.

Prayer: *Thank You Father God. I trust Your plan. I trust Your seasons for my life. And even in solitude, You know what's best for me. Enrich me Father. Teach me. Bless me. Add so much value to my life that I will have something to contribute that will bless others. Be glorified in me. In Jesus' name, Amen.*

(Read Isaiah 41:10)

Invest in your most important relationships.

"A man of too many friends comes to ruin, but there is a friend who sticks closer than a brother"
Proverbs 18:24, NASB.

꙳

You may have many acquaintances that you enjoy talking with, but when it comes to those real, genuine, we-bring-out-the-best-in-each other, and are always-there-for-each other friendships, you will only have a few.

These days' people collect friendships like they collect designer shoes. Each week, they have a new best friend. The moment something doesn't go their way they're on to the next friendship. But a quality and lasting relationship is not something you collect like shoes. It's someone that God brings into your life to help you become all that He created you to be. They may not be a perfect person, but they are a perfect gift from God that you are to care for, invest quality time in and preserve.

Here's a challenge for you...Make a list of the ten most important relationships in your life, from greatest to least. This can include your spouse, your mother, your grandmother, your sister, your close friend, etc. Next, look to see if whether you are investing the majority of your quality time in the relationships that you listed as most important to you.

Maybe you are spending more time with those who live near you because it's more convenient. But in order for any relationship to thrive and become all that God intended, you must invest quality time and attention to it. In the long-run, you will be much happier if you take the time to invest in the most meaningful relationships in your life.

Prayer: *Father God, thank you for Your wisdom. I receive it. Thank You for every relationship You have blessed me with. Help me never take them for granted. Help me bring out the best in the people in my life and help them bring out the best in me. Help these relationships thrive and be all that You purposed for them to be. In Jesus' name, Amen.*

You're a Jewel

*"Who can find a virtuous woman? for her price is
far above rubies."*
Proverbs 31:10

When someone abuses you, they don't see what God sees in you. When someone disrespects you, they don't see what God sees in you. And to be truthful, if you allow the abuse and the disrespect, you don't see what God sees in you.

In Proverbs 31:10, it is not merely focusing on the woman, but on the kind of man it takes to find this kind of woman. It takes a certain kind of guy to find you, see you and love you. You're asking, "Why won't he love me?" Well, he's not looking for a ruby; he's looking for a good time. When you're desperate to be loved or afraid to be alone, this will only attract heartbreak.

Receive God's love. Lose yourself in Him. Let God show you who you are in Christ. Let Him help you to see yourself the way He sees you. Let the treasure within you enrich you. When you do this, you won't settle for a guy that knows nothing about treasured gems, but you'll wait on the one that recognizes a jewel when he sees one and who knows how to treat you.

Prayer: *Father God, I thank You for speaking directly to my heart. I receive Your love and the man You have for me. Show me who I am in You. Help me see myself the way You see me. I don't want to be found by just anyone. Let Your man, Your son, find me and let me add value to his life and bless him. In Jesus name, Amen.*

Laugh, laugh, *laugh*.

"A joyful heart is good medicine, but a crushed spirit dries up the bones." Proverbs 17:22, ESV

♔

It is said that most successful comedians come from dysfunctional families. I believe that to be true. My family was dysfunctional, but I always knew I was loved. Even when my mother cut the cord to the TV because we were arguing over what channel to watch, I knew she loved me.

As a young girl there was a movie called "Child's Play" where a doll named "Chucky" goes around killing people. I had a similar doll that was life-sized. On one dark night, while lying in bed, my sister threw Chucky at me. I screamed so loud and kicked a hole in the doll's head. That's when I knew my legs are strong. And whenever I need to move any furniture around the house, I just lie on the floor and push it with my feet.

We women are strong. Many of us get our exercise while carrying ten bags of groceries to the door, because we refuse to make a second trip.

We are special to God. We love hard. We sacrifice so others can be happy. We always put ourselves last on the list, don't we? I think that is why our friendships are so important to us. Talking and laughing with friends is more than enough therapy for me. Yet, it's sad when a friendship breaks up. It's truly heartbreaking. I just look forward to going to heaven, because there is no division or misunderstandings where God is. We just have to get things right while we're here, because if you don't like Suzie anymore, God just might put your mansion right next door to hers for all eternity.

I tell you, no matter what you're going through right now, you have to be able to laugh at yourself, laugh at your struggles and laugh at your pain. With God's help, everything's going to be alright my sister!

Prayer: *Lord I thank You for giving me joy in my heart. Help me keep a sense of humor no matter what I'm dealing with and let it minister healing to my body. I don't want to shrivel up and die from anger and bitterness. I want to live, Lord. Change my countenance from mad to glad, from sour-full to powerful. I receive a flood of your joy and peace right now. Use me Lord to brighten someone's day today. In Jesus' name, Amen.*

Broken to Beautiful

"He himself bore our sins in his body on the tree, that we might die to sin and live to righteousness. By his wounds you have been healed" 1 Peter 2:24.

When my son has to clean up something off the floor, he often cries, "It's too much! This will take forever!" That's exactly how I felt when I hit rock bottom and my life shattered into a million tiny pieces. I thought it was too much for God and that His restoration of my life would take forever, but I was wrong.

No matter how broken your life may be, God knows how to put the broken pieces back together again. He can make it better than before. Know that your life is not beyond repair, it's not too much for God, and no, it will not take Him forever. God specializes in making all things new.

Keep moving forward and watch Him do what no man can do. Receive His healing and restoring love. Receive the truth that Jesus' body was broken so you can be made whole. What He has done for countless of others, He will surely do for you if you believe.

Prayer: *Father God, I cry out to you to heal everything that's broken in my life. Make all things new. I know you can do it because you've done it for others. Do it for me God. Bless me with miraculous restoration and use me to testify of your goodness everywhere I go. I yield to you now, and I pray that you are glorified in me. In the name of Jesus', Amen.*

(Read Revelation 21:5; Isaiah 61:3)

Just Dance

"...I came that they may have and enjoy life, and have it in abundance (to the full, till it overflows)."
John 10:10, Amplified

A few years ago I went salsa dancing with my husband. Before we hit the dance floor, I envisioned myself doing all the right moves, all the right twists and turns. In my mind, I was a national salsa dancing champion. We got on the floor and the music was just right, the mood was just right, my hubby was looking just right, but my hips were not moving just right. I could not make my body do what I was envisioning in my head. So finally I let go of all expectations and demands I had placed on myself, closed my eyes and just danced.

Just dance.

Your life may not be where you always

envisioned it would be just yet, but all you have is now. Remove the unrealistic expectations and unfair demands of perfection you've placed on yourself...close your eyes...and just dance. Really experience life. Really experience God's love. Enjoy the knowledge that you belong to the Lord and feel the joy of sharing Him with others. Enjoy the life God has given you as you cast every care on Him!

Prayer: *Father God, thank You for the life You have given me. Show me how to fully live it without placing demands of perfection on myself. Help me to just dance, just live, and enjoy the gift of life You've given me and live it to the full in You. In Jesus' name, Amen.*

I Will Not Be Moved

The storms come
to shake my faith
but I will not be moved
the winds blow
against my face
but I will not be moved
I will not move prematurely
going to wait for God to deliver me
though trouble is all around
there's a blessing to be found
so come what may
yes come what may
God has called me here
and here I will stay
I will not
no, I will not
be moved

"Consider it a sheer gift, friends, when tests and challenges come at you from all sides. You know that under pressure, your faith-life is forced into the

open and shows its true colors. So don't try to get out of anything prematurely. Let it do its work so you become mature and well-developed, not deficient in any way" James 1:2-4, The Message, MSG.

ꚍ

Maybe God is asking you to do something you've never done before. Maybe you are being tested like you've never been tested before. Just know that you're about to be blessed like you've never been blessed before. Don't be moved, God is working. You've come too far to give up now. There's a blessing after every trial, and there's treasure after every war.

Prayer: *Father God, I bless you. You know how to minister directly to my heart and to my situation. Thank you for being my rock and my Savior. I put my trust in you. Help me to stand fast and not be moved by anything I see, hear or feel. Help me to only be moved by you. In Jesus name, Amen.*

(Read Psalms 62:6)

A Comeback Child

"And we know that in all things God works for the good of those who love him, who have been called according to his purpose" Romans 8:28, NIV.

There are no shortcuts in the process in which God has to take us through in order to mature us spiritually. There may be some acceleration due to our faithfulness of embracing the process, but definitely no shortcuts. You might have experienced what some people call "setbacks", but they are really "set ups".

The enemy's intention is to "set you back" from keeping the faith, serving God, loving others, and believing in His purpose and plan for your life, etc. BUT GOD's intention is to "set you up" for a deeper level of intimacy and dependency, a deeper level of trust and hope, and a deeper level of self-examination and humility.

So don't despise the trails and

tribulations, because they're part of the "process" that you must undergo in order to be polished into a useful vessel for the Lord.

REPEAT AFTER ME: I am a comeback child and I will turn my "setbacks" into "comebacks".

Prayer: *Lord, I trust that You are for me and that every difficult situation that I experience that tries to knock me down is nullified by the blood of Your Son. I will rise and come back even stronger and wiser because of You. I Love You King Jesus, Amen!*

You Will Face Trials, But Be Encouraged

"I have told you all this so that you may have peace in me. Here on earth you will have many trials and sorrows. But take heart, because I have overcome the world" John 16:33, NLT.

♔

Real Christians face real trials. Once you believe in Jesus with your heart and confess Him with your mouth, you receive salvation, but that doesn't mean you won't go through anything. If you are facing a real challenge in your life don't think something is wrong with you or your salvation.

Maybe other Christians you see appear to be happy all of the time and look as if they aren't going through anything at all. That's not real! As long as you are in your fleshly body and living in this natural earthly realm, you will have many trials and tribulations. Your faith will be tried and what you believe will be put to the ultimate test. "But be of good cheer" Jesus said, "I have overcome the world." Take heart! Take courage! Believe God and His promises to you!

The Spirit of the living God lives within you and He will teach you how to overcome and how to walk victoriously. You can have peace in the storm, trusting that God has a divine plan for it all. He will use everything you've gone through to strengthen your faith muscles, and make you an even more powerful and effective witness for His glory!

Prayer: *Father God, thank You for encouraging me deeply today. No matter what I face, help me stay reminded that You are with me. Thank You for keeping me close to Your side and never letting me go. Thank You for teaching me Your truth and causing me to always triumph through Christ. I love You! In Jesus name, Amen.*

(Read 1 Corinthians 15:56-58; 2 Corinthians 2:14)

At the Feet of Jesus

"And she had a sister called Mary, which also sat at Jesus' feet, and heard his word" Luke 10:39.

"And great multitudes came unto him, having with them those that were lame, blind, dumb, maimed, and many others, and cast them down at Jesus' feet; and he healed them" Matthew 15:30.

Being at Jesus' feet is the most powerful place to be and the most needful. It is a place of worship and total surrender to God. In the days when Jesus walked the earth, no one left His feet with a need unmet, a body unhealed, a heart unloved, and a soul still possessed. They received what they came to Him for and so will you!

The enemy will stop at nothing to keep you from getting to the only One that can change everything about your life with one touch and with one Word. Be determined to stay at the feet of His presence and at the feet of His Word, receiving His instructions daily and looking for ways to apply what you read to your life. Everything you need to live victoriously is found at Jesus' feet.

Prayer: *Father God, I come to You realizing who I am without You. I'm nothing without You and I can do nothing apart from You. You are my God and I surrender my entire life to You. I love You. Take control of my life and make me new. In Jesus' name, Amen.*

The Ultimate Gift

*"Every good and perfect gift is from above,
and comes from the Father of lights,
with whom there is no variation or
shadow of turning"* James 1:17, NKJV.

It is customary in many cultures to receive presents during the holidays or on special occasions. We open our gift and are totally surprised. Then, there are times we may not care for the present at all and want to return it for something better.

God, in His unfailing love, sent His only Son Jesus as His "Ultimate Gift" to us. Never will we be able to understand fully that sacrifice or how important we are to God. We are priceless in His eyes and He makes no mistakes. Every day as we wake, we have the privilege and opportunity of unwrapping that gift of Jesus Christ. We get to enjoy an eternal relationship with our loving Savior. We get to share all of our ups and downs, successes and failures. The gift of Jesus is more than anything this world has to offer.

I am so grateful that God didn't trade me in when He saw the mess I had made of myself. Instead, He gave me beauty for ashes, and the oil of joy for mourning. Hallelujah!!!!

Let us rejoice in knowing that just as we have the "Ultimate Gift" of Jesus, we too are a beautiful and unique gift to and from the Father. We have the ability to go and be a gift to others.

Prayer: *Father I thank You for Your Son, Jesus. Sometimes I forget how blessed I am to have Him. I also don't realize the beautiful gift I am for You at times. Help me to see myself the way You see me. In Jesus name. Amen.*

(Read Isaiah 61:3; Ephesians 2:8; Romans 6:23; Psalm 139:14)

Integrity

"The righteous man walks in his integrity; his children are blessed after him"
Proverbs 20:7, NKJV.

Integrity is defined as the quality of being honest and having strong moral principles. The main question we all must ask ourselves is, "Am I a woman of integrity?" "Am I an honest person?" Only you know the answer.

When you don't lie on your paperwork, when you don't take more time on your lunch break than allowed, when you don't call in sick knowing you feel well, when you keep your commitments and stay true to your promises, when you don't try to justify or defend your wrong behavior but admit to the truth, this is all integrity.

A lack of integrity can cost you EVERYTHING. It can cost you your job and everything you worked hard to obtain. It can cost you the respect of your family and friends. It can cost you your witness and your ministry. It doesn't matter how strong the temptation may be, think about what it will cost you.

We have a responsibility as believers to walk in integrity before God. It's not so that man can look at you and say, oh isn't she amazing. It's so that God can be glorified through your life.

God will work in you the will and to do of His good pleasure (see Philippians 2:13). He will work in your heart and renew your mind. His motives are pure in wanting you to get this message in your heart. It is because He wants to bless you and make you a tremendous blessing in the earth.

Prayer: *Father God, work in me integrity of heart. Grow me up in godly character. I don't want to bring shame to Your name and cause You to be seen as anything else but holy. I want to glorify You publicly and in my private life. God! I cry out to You to help me be a woman of integrity consistently through Your grace and power. I just want to please You. In Jesus' name, Amen.*

No, You Need Peace

*"You will keep him in perfect peace, whose mind is
stayed on You, because he trusts in You"*
Isaiah 26:3, NKJV.

♕

Read this Scripture out loud and think on
how it applies to your life and your
situation.

I'll never forget a season in my life when
every time I went to the altar for prayer the
minister would tell me that I needed peace. I
would go to them and say, "I need prayer
for wisdom because I'm having to make
important decisions." They would look at
me and say, "No, you need peace." Then I
would go up to the altar again the next
Sunday-this time to a different person-
asking for prayer for my marriage and
family. Same response, "No, you need
peace." After this happened several times I
became frustrated because I thought I

already had peace. So I asked my husband, "Do I look peaceful to you?" He smiled and said, "No, you look like you always have a lot on your mind." I didn't have peace at all because my mind was on everything else but God.

Peace is more than a feeling, it's a knowing that everything is going to be alright because God is on your side. In every situation, you can trust in the Lord to make good on His promises to you. A sure indicator of trust in God is a fixed mind. It's not worrying how He is going to do it or when He will come through. It is being able to rest in your heart and soul because you know God loves you and He cares about every detail of your life.

Prayer: *Father God, I thank You for speaking to my heart. You are my faithful God and I love You! Help me to keep my mind stayed on You. Keep me in Your perfect peace. I can't do anything in my own strength. You are the only One who can do it. I put my total trust in You right now and I ask that You be glorified in my life. In Jesus name, Amen.*

Lend Them Your Key

"Each of you should use whatever gift you have received to serve others, as faithful stewards of God's grace in its various forms. If anyone speaks, they should do so as one who speaks the very words of God. If anyone serves, they should do so with the strength God provides, so that in all things God may be praised through Jesus Christ. To him be the glory and the power forever and ever. Amen."

1 Peter 4:10-11, NIV

Keys are used to lock and unlock things we possess that hold some type of perceived value. As a result, we tend to take special care of the key and in some instances, secure a back-up. But did you know that a key is stored within us each time God reveals himself to us in His Word? If you don't believe me, sit in a room with other women and listen to them share their "story", their "key".

Daughters, it is healthy for us to share what God has done in our lives with one another. We are his mouth-piece to the world. We are his mouth-piece to one another. Lies are eradicated in our heart when we listen to the testimony of another person who went through the same thing that we went through and came out on the other side better than before. Hope is created when we share the keys that our sweet Lord has given us.

So don't hesitate and don't shrink back when He presents an opportunity for you to share your story. Lend them your key.

Prayer: *Father, I have been so distracted by the concerns of my own heart that I have failed to be a witness to the people in your heart. Thank you for reminding me that you gave us Your Word so that we would share it with those who need it. Your Word is my key and I choose to share it. In Jesus' name, Amen!*

A Clear View

*"Wherefore seeing we also are compassed about with
so great a cloud of witnesses, let us lay aside every
weight, and the si which doth so easily beset us, and
let us run with patience the race that is set before us,
looking unto Jesus the author and finisher of our
faith; who for the joy that was set before him
endured the cross, despising the shame,
and is set down at the right hand
of the throne of God"* Hebrews 12:1-2.

♔

One morning when I woke up, I tried to
look at the time, but a glass cup was in the
way. I tried to see the numbers on the clock,
but they were blurred by an obstacle. God
spoke to my heart and said there are many
who can't see Me and My plans because
they're vision is blurred by obstacles as small
as a glass cup. It took nothing for me to
pick up the cup and move it out of my way.

God wants us to see His heart and
see His plans for our lives, but we have to

lay aside, push aside and move from our way every obstacle and every weight. I speak clear vision over your life right now in Jesus name! A clear view! Nothing distorted or blurred! See God in His glory. See people with right eyes. Move the obstacle so you can see yourself properly and respond properly to the situations in your life.

Prayer: *Father God, thank You for Your encouragement. I receive these words in my heart and I ask you to help me. Help me to move out of my way any sin and any obstacle that is causing me to not see things right. Work in me Lord and help me to have a clear view. In Jesus' name, Amen.*

Get on the Highway of Faith

"For in it the righteousness of God is revealed from faith to faith; as it is written, "The just shall live by faith" Romans 1:17, NKJV.

When you're going down a Fearful Road, get off at the next exit and get on the Highway of Faith.

The Fearful Road only takes you down, down, down. The moment you get on it, you immediately know that something doesn't feel right. You no longer recognize your surroundings and everything looks darker and darker. That's when you must make a decision to get off that road and get on the Highway of Faith.

The Faith Highway doesn't go down or grow darker the longer you drive. It goes up and up, and everything gets brighter and brighter. Joy rises in your heart, and you find yourself singing praise to God.

So how do you get on the Highway of Faith? You first recognize that you are not going the right way. Ask yourself, "What am I running from?" "What am I choosing not to do because I feel afraid?" Then you do that particular thing that God is prompting you to do. That one simple act of obedience will get you on Faith's Highway to a life that goes higher and higher in the Lord. This is the way you become stronger in your faith, by not running or hiding in fear, but choosing to live by faith and in love. This is the only way to truly live.

Prayer: *Father God, I receive Your words to my heart. Thank You for speaking to me in such a way that I can understand it. You love me and I love You. Help me not to go down the road of fear, but to stay on the highway of faith. Help my faith in You to win over every feeling I have. I don't want to go down, I want to climb higher and higher in You. In Jesus name, Amen.*

You can never love anyone you're envious of.

"...love never is envious nor boils over with jealousy..." 1 Corinthians 13:4, Amplified.

Envy is defined as to have warm feelings for or against. It's the emotion that comes over you when you see someone enjoying something that you don't have.

Envy starts as a seed of thought and can turn into a complex root system in the heart that can take over someone's mind. If left alone, envy and jealousy will germinate into hatred, strife and division. It's what motivates murders and evil of every kind. Envy can cause you to try to sabotage someone's life, their relationships, their ministry and their name.

The lie the enemy tells us is that someone has something that we can't have. Don't listen to the whispers and taunts of the enemy. God will bring you through whatever situation you're in and can bring you to a place of victory. You don't have to be envious of anyone of God's children because He loves us all the same. What He does for one; He will do for you if you trust and obey Him.

Understand that when someone is winning in life, you are only seeing their fruit, and the end result of a lot of sacrifice, sweat and tears. Anyone that you see is very blessed, know that they went through major tests and trials to get where they are. Love them and bless them.

If you're struggling with envy and burning with jealousy, stop everything you're doing right now and pray this prayer...

Father God, I repent for being envious of _____(person's name)_____. Forgive me God. I reject every lie of the enemy and I ask that You pull up every root of envy and bitterness in my heart. I pray You bless the people in my life that are successful. Cause them to experience more success. Protect them Lord and keep them from falling. Be glorified in my life and in theirs. In Jesus name, Amen.

(Read Romans 13:13; 2 Corinthians 12:20; Galatians 5:21, Galatians 5:26; Philippians 1:15; 1 Timothy 6:4; Titus 3:3; James 3:14-16, James 4:5; 1 Peter 2:1)

Be Accountable

"Iron sharpeneth iron; so a man sharpeneth the countenance of his friend." Proverbs 27:17

A life that is deficient in iron will cause one to become physically weak. Likewise, a relationship that is iron deficient, where no one is being sharpened, corrected, or provoked to good works is not beneficial to growth. People may fear upsetting you or hurting your feelings, but a real friend that loves you would much rather make you upset and please God instead of the other way around.

Accountability isn't telling people what to do. It is encouraging them to do what God has already instructed them to do. We are not just helping each other stay out of sin, but helping one another move forward into being all that God created us to be. We will never grow on an island isolated away from people. Nor will we grow if we surround ourselves only with those that think like us and talk like us. We need people that get up under our skin and irritate us, encouraging us to grow and mature. Not "yes" people, but those who feel personally responsible to help us become all that God has called us to be.

Prayer: *Father God, I need more iron in my life. I pray that You send true friends that will not appease me, but will sharpen me and help me be what You called me to be. I thank You for always knowing what's best for me. In Jesus' name, Amen.*

Knitted Hearts

Part 1

"As soon as he had finished speaking to Saul, the soul of Jonathan was knit to the soul of David, and Jonathan loved him as his own soul."
1 Samuel 18:1, ESV.

♔

I love the story of David and Jonathan. As we see in our opening verse, God sometimes knits hearts together, like He did with them, and He puts people in our path because He knows we'll need them. Godly friendships are a wonderful force to be reckoned with. He uses our friendships as vessels, to encourage and strengthen one another. Jonathan loved David, believed in him, and sought God's best for him. Jonathan's friendship was what David needed to grow into the king and leader he was to become.

Friendships are vital in our walk with Christ because, in them, we are sharpened and are held accountable by one another. It's not about your win in this race; it's about a corporate win that makes this journey worthwhile. In Ecclesiastes 4:9-10 it says: "Two are better than one, because they have a good return for their labor: if either of them falls down, one can help the other up. But pity anyone who falls and has no one to help them up."

Truth: Never underestimate the power of two hearts knit together for God's purpose.

Point to Ponder: If you desire this type of friendship, are you leading by example?

Pray with me: *Dear Heavenly Father, thank You for the gift of friendships. Lord, please surround me with strong friendships that will add value to my life, and I pray I can do the same for them. Thank You Lord, because You have heard my prayer and You are already working behind the scenes. In Jesus name I pray, Amen!*

(Read Proverbs 27:17)

Knitted Hearts

Part 2

*"As soon as he had finished speaking to Saul,
the soul of Jonathan was knit to the
soul of David, and Jonathan loved him
as his own soul"* 1 Samuel 18:1, ESV.

In the midst of corrupted hearts, authentic, non-competitive, loving friendships do exist, but only God can supply such a thing. I didn't always have this mindset, especially after some friendship betrayals, but once I drew closer to God and allowed Him to work in my heart, I began to attract what I gave.

If you give love, you'll receive love! If you have compassion, you'll receive compassion! If you encourage, you'll receive plenty of encouragement! If you offer support, God will surround you with loving supporters! We call this, "sowing and reaping." You can't expect to receive what you never give.

Beyond common interests and a sense of humor, the aim of friendships are to sow into each other words of purpose, eternal life and blessings. When we do this, we refresh each other's spirit and strengthen each other's faith. A Godly friendship means you bear your own hurts along with those of your friend. You cry when they cry, laugh when they laugh, applaud them when they succeed and hold up their arms when the battle has made them weak.

Truth: You can't expect to receive what you never give.

Point to Ponder: Are you being the kind of friend you want to have?

Pray with me: *Dear Heavenly Father, I ask that You heal every wound from past failed friendships. I deeply desire to have true friendships in my life, but I know I have to give in order to receive. So I pray that You help me be the Godly friend You expect me to be. In Jesus name I pray, Amen!*

A Father to the Fatherless

"Sing praises to God and to his name! Sing loud praises to him who rides the clouds. His name is the Lord-rejoice in his presence! Father to the fatherless, defender of widows-this is God, whose dwelling is holy" Psalm 68:4-5, NLT.

꒰♕꒱

As a little girl, I didn't get to experience the love of a natural father. I don't have the memories that so many women have of their dads when they were small. It wasn't until my early adolescent years that God would bring a special someone into my mother's life that would be a father to me and would love me as his own. I know what it's like to feel abandoned, and I know what it's like to be found.

Maybe you never knew the love of a father. Today, God wants you to know that He loves you and You are dear and precious to Him. You don't have to search anymore. The love you long for is found in Him. His love far exceeds the love any person can offer you. Receive His love and He will show you what a real father and daughter relationship is.

Prayer: *Father God, thank You for being a great and loving Father to me. You affirm me and make me feel so safe and secure. I reach out to You to pick me up and love me. I receive You and Your love, Your special care and Your words spoken over me. I receive You as my Father and Your amazing love. In Jesus' name, Amen.*

(Read 2 Corinthians 6:18)

What it Means to Seek

"Seek the Lord while you can find him. Call on him now while he is near" Isaiah 55:6, New Living Translation, NLT.

The Hebrew definition for the word "seek" is to tread or frequent; usually to follow (for pursuit or search); by implication to seek or ask; specifically to worship. In the English Dictionary, to seek is to attempt to find (something).

The reason there aren't many seekers of the Lord is because we have the wrong perspective of what it means to seek. Our seeking is more than an attempt to find something. It is how we worship; it is a full persuasion that God is who He said He is, and He will do everything He promised He will do.

The truth is, every Christian isn't seeking God. Just because you are praying doesn't mean you are seeking God. To seek is to frequent God's company and search His Word for wisdom and direction until you receive what He has promised you. It is constantly asking, "OK Lord, I did step one. Now, what is step two? OK, I've obeyed You here. Now, what do You want me to do next?" It is constantly checking in with Him to navigate you to the victory He's promised you.

Prayer: *Father God, thank You for Your divine insight. I ask that you give me the heart of a seeker. I don't know everything and I can't get to Your promises for my life without You directing me and instructing my heart. Help me to get this message in my heart and cause Your truth to produce visible results in my life. In Jesus name, Amen.*

(Read Isaiah 45:19; 1Chronicles 28:9; 2Chronicles 19:3; Job 8:5; Psalms 14:2, Psalms 27:8)

Loose Them and Let Them Go

*"The thief's purpose is to steal and kill and destroy.
My purpose is to give them a rich and satisfying life"*
John 10:10, New Living Translation.

When an eagle swoops down to pick up a fish from the water, if it holds on to a fish that is too big for too long, the eagle risks being drowned by a fish.

Are you refusing to let go of someone and drowning in the process? It doesn't matter who the person may be and what they've meant to you in the past, if God has instructed you to let them go while He does His work, let them go.

This is how the enemy destroys a life. He entices you to hold on to, run after, obsess over, and completely lose yourself in your hunt for a fish. Loose them and let them go so you can soar the way God intended for you to soar. You may can't imagine life without them, but now is the time to obey His prompting lest you drown.

Prayer: *Father God, thank You for speaking directly to my heart. Forgive me for trying to hold on to someone you've told me to let go of. I repent for placing a person before You. I yield to You right now and to Your will. I trust You know what's best for me. Take Your rightful place on the throne of my heart and help me move forward. In Jesus name', Amen.*

A Quiet Confidence

"For thus says the Lord God, the Holy One of Israel: "In returning and rest you shall be saved; In quietness and confidence shall be your strength." But you would not" Isaiah 30:15, NKJV.

When an eagle knows he will need his energy for the hunt, he rests quietly-preserving his energy. We are at our strongest when we are quiet and confident. The assignment God has for you to accomplish will require all of you, engaged and ready. Don't exert energy trying to articulate all that God has shown you to those around you. Don't spend all of your time trying to get the approval of man. Don't give much thought toward how it will happen for you.

You can have quiet assurance and a joyful expectation when you know it's truly from God. Every promise from His word is true. The One that has called you is faithful.

He will do it. As you make preparations to walk in your destiny, and as you prepare for the hunt, rest quietly dear. Tell only what God instructs you to share, as you let God's hand on your life and His move in your heart speak for themselves.

Prayer: *Father God, I thank You for Your rich words to me. I receive it, I believe it, and I will see it. Help me to rest quietly while You lead me into Your destiny for my life. I want to be a doer, not a talker. Help me stay focused on You and Your promises. Be glorified in me. In Jesus name, Amen.*

(Read 1 Thessalonians 5:24)

Confidence.

"Being confident of this very thing, that he which hath begun a good work in you will perform it until the day of Jesus Christ" Philippians 1:6, KJV.

♔

Being confident is the terminology used by the Apostle Paul and penned by Timothy while sitting in a dark, filthy dungeon. He wrote to the church at Philippi. And though his external conditions grew worse, he was becoming increasingly confident, convinced and inwardly certain that what God had started in them, He would complete.

It is the nature of God to allow you to face tough situations to bring out the best in you. It is only in tests and trials that we discover that God truly lives in us. It is only when someone accuses you of being something you're not, that you open your Bible to find who you truly are in Him. Our being reassured by Him increases our confidence.

Don't allow that negative situation to cause you to become deflated and discouraged. You may be ready to head for the hills, but God says to, "Look to the hills from whence comes your help. Your help comes from the Lord" (see Psalm 121:1-2).

Declare this today from your heart:

"The Lord God is my Strength, my personal bravery, and my invincible army; He makes my feet like hinds' feet and will make me to walk [not to stand still in terror, but to walk] and make [spiritual] progress upon my high places [of trouble, suffering, or responsibility]!" Habakkuk 3:19, Amplified

Prayer: *Father God, I thank You for speaking to my heart so clearly. I have lost confidence, but I ask You to please restore it. Make me strong and full of confidence in You. In Jesus name, Amen.*

God Has Greater in Mind

"Verily, verily, I say unto you, He that believes on me, the works that I do shall he do also; and greater works than these shall he do; because I go unto my Father" John 14:12, KJV.

ꙮ

No weakness, insecurity, set back, or negative words spoken over you is strong enough to stop God's great and preordained plans for your life. When He called you, He already knew every mistake you were going to make and every giant you would have to face. You've been called for such a time as this. There is a reason you survived when others around you didn't, a reason you are still standing and are still here.

Receive in your heart God's great plans for your life and the great work He has called you to do, even if you can't fully wrap your mind around it. Just know that

He is preparing you for greater. Greater levels of faith, greater operations of the gifts of the Spirit, greater manifestations of healing and power, greater knowledge and awareness of who He is, and a greater deeper walk with Him.

Prayer: *Father, You are so great and awesome. I put my trust in You. Whatever you want to do, I yield. Take me higher than I've ever gone before. When life becomes challenging for me, help me remember that the Greater One lives within me. You've called me to do great things, and I accept it now. In Jesus' name, Amen.*

He is thinking about you.

"You will keep him in perfect peace, whose mind is stayed on You, because he trusts in You"
Isaiah 26:3, NKJV.

God can use anything and anyone to remind you that He is with you. He'll use the ray of the sunshine on your face, the warm hug from your grandchild, the blossoming flowers on your porch and the unexpected check in the mail. He has special ways to let you know, He is thinking about you. God created thoughtfulness. It is what He is. You are on His mind constantly, and it's the good and healthy kind of obsession.

What if you made it your personal pursuit to think about God just as much as He thinks about you? It is not hard to do if you consider a romantic relationship. When you really like someone, that person consumes your thoughts. They are on your mind when you wake up and when you lie down to go to sleep. You daydream at work because you're planning your wedding, and the person hasn't even asked you out on a date. We know how to think about someone all through the day. Imagine how much peace you'll experience if you trained your mind to think about God that way.

Challenge: As you go throughout your day, and as you observe everything around you, look for how those things remind you of God's nature and how He feels about you.

Prayer: *Father God, I thank You for speaking to my heart. Thank You for thinking of me and loving me the way You do. Help me to think about You the same way. You deserve that. You've done so much for me. I'm sorry for being so distracted with cares. Change my heart and mind to be more focused and centered on You. In Jesus name, Amen.*

(Read Psalm 139)

If you trust Me, I will...

⚜

What would it take for you to doubt God's love? Take a moment and ponder that question.

For many of us, it doesn't take much. Just a small amount of adversity and we are offended with God and ready to give up on Him. We don't understand why He let it happen, and it makes us afraid to trust Him.

We don't want to hear He loves us, because to us, if He truly loved us, He would do something about our situation. Our minds are consumed with, "If He loved me, He would do something about this." But God's mind is focused on, "I do love you, and if you trust Me, I will do something." If you trust and believe, He will keep His promise to you!

Understand that God's not intimidated by your anger with Him. So many of us are angry with God when He's not the problem. Our lack of trust is the problem. We're not fully persuaded, and to be quite honest, we don't believe. In this hour, we must be fully persuaded and confident in the love God has for us like never before. We must be confident that He has a plan for our lives and His plans are good. If we trust Him, He will do what He promised He will do.

Maintain your glow. Maintain the gleam in your eyes. Maintain the joy in your stride. Don't stop talking about the goodness of your God and His amazing grace. Don't sit down in defeat, get up and give God the glory! He will escort you to victory!

Prayer: *Father God, I thank You for speaking directly to my heart these words of life. You are so faithful to me. Help me to be faithful to You. Help me maintain my glow and my shine for You, no matter what I face. Father, You love me and I put my trust in You. I rejoice that You will see me through to victory. In Jesus' mighty name, Amen.*

(Read Job 40)

A Kingdom Sisterhood

Part 1

"But Ruth replied, "Don't urge me to leave you or to turn back from you. Where you go I will go, and where you stay I will stay. Your people will be my people and your God my God" Ruth 1:16, NIV.

As Christian women, we have a tremendous opportunity to impact the lives of those women around us; with love, support, encouragement, words of wisdom and compassion. To have a true love for sisterhood is a beautiful thing. Unfortunately nowadays, there is so much envy, competition and jealousy that we don't find the freedom to be who we are with those around us.

There is something to be said about women helping women. It speaks volumes when we are like-minded, when we deeply understand each other's joys and challenges within our unique lifestyles, when we are truly full of joy with our sister's achievements in Christ, and when we celebrate eachother and take pride in being a part of that growth.

It glorifies God when we are women who are there as accountability partners, understanding that you may have flaws but loving you anyway; understanding that you will fall many times but holding you up anyway; understanding that you're not perfect but seeing you through the perfect eyes of Christ anyway! It pleases Him when we are women who pray fervently for you just as we would desire for someone to pray for us, when we don't judge or criticize, but correct in love when needed, and women who push you towards your destiny with words of hope and courage.

As Christian women, we must return to this quality kind of sisterhood, and we must do it for the Lord's name.

Prayer: *Heavenly Father, thank You for the gift of sisterhood. Thank You for those women that surround me. I pray that I am able to offer them the type of friendship that pleases You; a friendship like the one of Jonathan and David and like the one of Ruth and Naomi. I pray that You always help me lead by example and I pray that I am able, through You, to impact the lives of those around me. In Jesus name I pray, Amen.*

A Kingdom Sisterhood
Part 2

"But Ruth replied, "Don't urge me to leave you or to turn back from you. Where you go I will go and where you stay I will stay. Your people will be my people and your God my God" Ruth 1:16, NIV.

࿈

As we read in Titus 2, women who help women usually produce wisdom and achievements. When we stick together, we begin strong, accelerate fast and finish well. The Bible teaches us that when two or more are gathered together in the same Spirit, God is amongst them. Let's be women of the same Spirit. Let's be women of change and impact. It is God's desire to see women work together in love and for one purpose, which is to lift His name high.

I love the story of Ruth and Naomi because it shows what sisterhood is all about; a love that is not separated by anything, a love that conquers all together, a union that is inseparable. Although this is something we would all love to have, we must always remember to be that person to someone else first. We must never forget that the rule of life is reaping what we sow; we can't expect to receive from others what we've never sown into them. We are called to stand out in every area of our lives, especially when it comes to relationships because the focal point of a Christian life is the relationship we have with our Father.

Healthy relationships are essential, so who are you impacting today? Who are you pouring yourself into today? Who are you are supporting and loving today; because who you are matters and it speaks volumes. Don't lead by words, lead by example!

Prayer: *Heavenly Father, I thank You for speaking to my heart regarding the importance of sisterhood. When the enemy wants me to turn inward, help me to turn outward. When he wants me to give up on sisterhood because of past hurts, help me push to have Your view. I pray that I am able to help women in my life see themselves the way*

*You see them and know that they are loved by You.
In Jesus name I pray, Amen!*

(Read Titus 2:3-5)

You were designed to reach women.

"This is the message we have heard from Him and announce to you, that God is Light, and in Him there is no darkness at all. If we say that we have fellowship with Him and yet walk in the darkness, we lie and do not practice the truth" 1 John 1:5-6, NASB.

You were designed to reach women, not to sleep with them. The arms of a woman were designed to pull you up from your lowest place, help you along your way, and hug you when you need comfort, but never to be a lover's embrace for you.

For some, they have suffered much, and have been abused at the hands of a man that was supposed to help protect them. They longed for affection, and the enemy turned a pure desire for love into a perverted pursuit. Then there are those whose desire didn't come from an abusive past or a life void of love and affection; they simply wanted her.

What do you do when you want what God hates? How do you reach inside yourself and turn that desire off? You can't do anything in your own power or strength. It is God Who works in us the will and to do of His good pleasure.

In the beginning the earth was void, and darkness covered the face of the deep, but God spoke saying, "Let there be light!" and there was light that dispelled all darkness. Jesus is powerful Light that dispels all darkness in our lives. When you give Him real access into your heart, He will flood your heart with His love and His light. You will begin to see Him as He is, see yourself as He sees you, and you will see the enemy for the deceiver he is.

The enemy wants you to stay bound so that you can not do the works God designed you to do. But today is your day to be free through Jesus if you so choose. His mercy and grace covers every area of our lives, not to conceal, but to free us from within, so we can live out His true design for our lives.

Prayer: *Father God, it's no secret to You what my inner struggles are. I am helpless, and I need You like I've never needed You before. Forgive me for every sin I've committed. Change my heart. Change my desires. Change my life. Flood me with Your light and remove even the memory of sinful pleasure, remove the taste from my mouth. I denounce the spirit of lust and sexual perversion, and I yield my spirit, soul, and body to You and You alone. Consecrate me, God. Wash me and purify me. Be glorified in my life. In Jesus name, Amen.*

(Read 1 Corinthians 6:9-11; 1 Corinthians 6:18; Genesis 1:3; Philippians 2:13; 1 John 1:9)

Get the Facts

"Finally, brothers and sisters, whatever is true, whatever is noble, whatever is right, whatever is pure, whatever is lovely, whatever is admirable—If anything is excellent or praiseworthy—think about such things." Philippians 4:8, NIV.

♔

It happens to be that 99.9% of the time, whenever we assume something, our assumptions are usually wrong. We can think, "He walked by me because...", "She didn't respond because...", or "They didn't invite me over because..." When we assume we are making judgments without knowing the real facts. Assumptions can keep our minds preoccupied all throughout the day, and if we aren't careful we will create emotions about something that hasn't been proven to be true. Assumptions are usually negative and can send a harmful message to our physical body. Our body doesn't know the difference between an assumption and a fact and will respond as if everything it feels is real.

Maybe they didn't invite you over because they forgot. Maybe she didn't respond because her life has been extremely busy lately. Maybe he walked by you because he was focused on getting somewhere on time and didn't see you. Everything people do to you is not because they don't like you or because they feel something negative about you. Love believes the best. Don't let assumptions ruin you. If you feel it's important to know something, it is wise to ask. We can't think on "whatever is true" if we don't know what is true. We must get the facts so we can have peace of mind.

Prayer: *Father God, my mind has been bogged down with assumptions. I assume everything without knowing anything. I find that my assumptions have usually been wrong. Help me learn to reject any thought that the enemy tries to plant in my mind about someone or something. Help me think on whatever is true. Give me peace of mind. In Jesus name, Amen.*

Tried with Fire

"That the trial of your faith, being much more precious than of gold that perisheth, though it be tried with fire, might be found unto praise and honour and glory at the appearing of Jesus Christ"
1 Peter 1:7.

The enemy may be bringing everything he has against you. Hurt after hurt. Calamity after calamity. Distress after distress. And while it feels as though you are not going to make it, your faith will. Your faith will see you through every single trial.

Just when you think you're done and can't take anymore, the Lord will show up and His grace will kick in. He is a very present help in time of trouble. He will fight for you. When He said He will never leave you nor forsake you, He meant it. When He said, He is your Shield and your Defense, He meant it. When He said that no weapon formed against you would prosper, He meant it. God hasn't abandoned you, and He has not left your side. He is right there to help your faith remain.

Understand that every Word of God strengthens your faith, so don't close your Bible now. Hide it in your heart and declare it from your mouth. Speak to your situation as you stand still and see the salvation of the Lord!

Prayer: *Father God, I cry out to You. You are my God and there is none else. Thank You for being my impenetrable Shield. I place my total trust in You. Every test, distress, and the fiery situation may be hard to bear, but You are with me to help me come through it victoriously. Thank You that Your Word fights for me. I hide it in my heart and declare it from my mouth. In Jesus name, Amen.*

Don't waste your life.

"But by the grace of God I am what I am, and His grace toward me was not in vain; but I labored more abundantly than they all, yet not I, but the grace of God which was with me"
1 Corinthians 15:10, NKJV.

Don't waste your life by being negative. Life is a precious gift from God. Things may not always go the way you want them to, but you must focus on the good rather than the bad. See life as a gift from God and live each day like it's your last.

Don't waste the gifts God has given you. The person that buried their talent were afraid, but it wasn't the right kind of fear. True reverence and fear for God will cause you to speak up even if your voice shakes, it will cause you to take the leap even if you see no way it will work.

Don't waste the relationships God has placed in your life. What you respect and honor will move toward you. What you disrespect and dishonor will move away from you. Every single relationship God has given you has a divine purpose. While you have them in your life, learn what they can teach you and enjoy them for who they are.

Don't waste the grace God has given you. When God reveals to you a tiny glimpse of His purpose for your life, there's grace to do what He has showed you. Do what you can with what's in your hands, and God will cause all grace to abound toward you. You have everything you need to fulfill God's divine purpose for your life.

Prayer: *Father God, thank You for speaking directly to my heart. I'm sorry for being wasteful. I know everything You've given me is from Your loving and gracious heart. Help me not to waste anything, but to use it all for Your glory. In Jesus' name, Amen.*

(Read Matthew 25:14-30; 2 Corinthians 9:8)

When You Pray For Your Friends

"And the LORD turned the captivity of Job, when he prayed for his friends: also the LORD gave Job twice as much as he had before"
Job 42:10.

♔

Maybe she didn't respond the way you wanted her to respond. She wasn't considerate and didn't seem to care for you as much as you care for her. Pray for her. You gave him your heart, and he walked all over it. He didn't do everything he promised. Pray for him. They loved you when you had something to give them, but now they seem to get some sick pleasure out of seeing you no longer on top and successful like you use to be. Pray for them.

Pray for every friend in your life, both old and new. For where God is taking you, you can't afford to have bitterness and resentment in your heart toward anyone.

When Job prayed for his friends, the Lord turned his situation around. God gave him twice as much wealth as he had before. It is the Lord that will turn things around for you when you wise up and do what big girls do. As you pray, God will bless you richly with a release and will turn things around for you.

Prayer: *Father God, I pray You help me with this. I've been disappointed by people who I considered my friends, and now I bring my heart to You. Heal me God and help me pray for them from a right place. With the faith and love of Jesus, I forgive them. I ask that You bless them Lord with Your mercy and grace. Give every friend in my life, old and new, a heart to know You more. Protect their families and place them in Your perfect will for their lives. In Jesus' name, Amen.*

Grace is the Necessary Ingredient for Your Success

"I do not frustrate the grace of God: for if righteousness come by the law, then Christ is dead in vain" Galatians 2:21.

If you are going to accomplish anything in the kingdom of God, it will be by the grace of God. It is the necessary ingredient for any real success. Trying to live apart from grace is like trying to hold your breath for a long time—you eventually faint.

God wants you to receive His abounding grace that is given to you through Jesus. At your lowest point, you need the grace of God to remind you of who you are in Christ. Then you need God's grace to help you pick up speed, spread your wings and soar. And while soaring, you need

God's grace to not crash, but remain in the air, going from glory to glory until you enter eternal glory.

There's never a moment in your life when you will not need God's supernatural strength and His favor on your life. His grace is enough for you. Don't think it is not. Don't look for man to do what only God's grace can do for you. It is your stability when you feel unstable. It is your strength when you feel weak. It is your humility when you are in pride. It is your wisdom when you don't understand. It is your memory of good when all you see around you is bad.

God will always challenge you to face your fears, to get outside of your comfort zone, and to deal with the most difficult personalities, to keep you constantly pulling on His grace.

Prayer: *Father God, thank You for speaking to me about the amazing grace I have in You. I receive it all because I need it. I need Your grace to help me do what You've purposed me to do. I need it to be*

*my strength and my confidence. Thank You Lord.
Cause Your grace to abound toward me. In Jesus
name, Amen.*

(Read 2 Timothy 2:1; 1 Corinthians 15:10;
Romans 5:2; 2 Corinthians 9:8)

Watch Your Words

*"The tongue can bring death or life; those who love
to talk will reap the consequences"*
Proverbs 18:21

👑

While talking to a friend, she wanted God to save her marriage. So we prayed together and a few days later, she came to me saying how frustrated she was and how she wanted out. I told her to get some duct tape and put it over her mouth because she was messing up what God wanted to do in her home with her words. In one breath it was, "Lord save my relationship." In another breath it was, "This man is the devil! I'm out of here!"

Well maybe you're in a relationship with someone that acts like the devil, or maybe your boss or parent behaves like the devil, and you don't know what to do. You want to see a change, but you don't think you have the patience or strength to wait it out while God does whatever He's going to do. In this situation, understanding is needed. The Bible says understanding will keep you (see Proverbs 2:11). It will help keep your tongue, and it will keep your mind.

Understanding is God's mind on the matter. Let Him show you what He thinks about the situation you're in and what He wants you to do.

Prayer: *Father God, thank You for speaking directly to my heart. I repent for the things I've been saying. Give me understanding and help me keep my mouth. Help me not cancel my prayers through wrong talking. Be glorified in this situation. I'll cooperate with You. In Jesus name, Amen.*

(Read James 1:5-7)

God wants to teach you how to live.

"The thief does not come except to steal, and to kill, and to destroy. I have come that they may have life, and that they may have it more abundantly" John 10:10, NKJV.

꩜

We all know how to die, but God wants to teach us how to live. We know how to crash, but God wants to show us how to soar in Him. Maybe you don't know what a real life in God looks like for you. What does freedom look like when you've been bound for so long? What is a prosperous life when you've been broke for so long? What does a happy life look like when you've been sad and depressed for so long? And what is true love when you've been abused since you were a little girl.

Maybe you've never experienced life as God has it, but that won't stop Him from giving it to you. His divine will is that you experience life and life more abundantly right here on earth. Abundant means superabundant in quality or superior in quality-the best life.

There is far more to life than what you've been experiencing. There's more to see, more to do, more to partake of and enjoy. Don't refuse the life He wants to give you just because you've never had it. He wants to fill your life with good things! He is good, and you have to trust in His goodness and love for you.

It is the divine responsibility of the Holy Spirit to lead and guide you into all truth. He will reveal His heart and will teach you how to live!

Prayer: *Father God, thank You for speaking directly to my heart. It can be scary pursuing what I've never had before. I don't know what it's like to truly live. Help me learn. Teach me, Lord, how to live. In Jesus name, Amen.*

(Read John 16:13; Ephesians 3:20-21)

You are Victorious

"Now thanks be to God who always leads us in triumph in Christ, and through us diffuses the fragrance of His knowledge in every place"
2 Corinthians 2:14, NKJV.

If you are victorious, that means someone is defeated. If you win, someone has lost. Every time you acknowledge the victory you have in Christ, God rises in your life, and the enemy flees in every direction. The Bible tells us, "Let the redeemed of the Lord say so." Who are the redeemed? Those who have been bought and purchased with the precious blood of Jesus. His sacrifice for them brings them into a perfect union with God Himself, and they are His. They are victorious because Jesus is victorious.

You may not feel like a winner, and your situation may not look at all victorious right now, but neither did Jesus look victorious nailed to a Cross. Your victory rests not in how much money is in your account or in how much food is in your fridge. Even when you're sitting in a dark room because the power has been turned off, you are still victorious in Christ. Things may look bad now, but just as Jesus rose in victory, so will you! You can go ahead, rejoice now and shout the victory because you are victorious through Christ and the devil is defeated!

Prayer: *Father God, thank You for the victory I have in You. My situation may not look like I've won anything, but I choose not to go by what I see or don't see. I trust the victory You've given me through Christ, and I choose to walk in it no matter how I feel or what I face. You have given me the victory, and now I'm good. I'm content. In Jesus name, Amen.*

Let Them Talk

"No weapon that is formed against thee
shall prosper; and every tongue that shall
rise against thee in judgment thou shalt
condemn. This is the heritage of the
servants of the LORD, and their
righteousness is of me, saith the LORD"
Isaiah 54:17.

☙

In the world today, many seem to be
obsessed with what others think and say
about them. They will allow these comments
to dictate their mood for the entire day and
influence future decisions. This may be true
for those in the world, but not so for a
daughter of the King. I say, let them talk.

The scripture above explains what
will happen to any tongue that rises against
you in judgment. The person who uses their
tongue in judgment against you will be
proven wrong. As you go about your life
living it for the LORD others will see and

be inspired to follow your God. They will look at you and wonder how you can have so much peace surrounded by a stressed out world. Others will hide and wait to see if what you are believing God for will actually come to pass in your life. There may be some who will attempt to set traps of failure and defeat for you to fall into which will ultimately trap the one who set it. Regardless of what others do, your confidence is in God.

You can live a fearless life free in Him with the revelation of the scripture above. So, do not be concerned with what others say or do not say. Do not be concerned with the number of "likes" your post or picture gets. Only be concerned with what Your Father thinks about you and know all of His thoughts toward you are good! (Jeremiah 29:11)

Prayer: *Dear Heavenly Father, I repent for being overly concerned about what others say or think about me. I receive your promise that no weapon formed against me shall prosper and any tongue that rises against me shall be condemned. This promise is my heritage, I am your servant and my righteousness is of You. Thank you Lord I can live fearlessly in You! In Jesus' Name I pray, Amen.*

You're Doing a Great Job!

"And let us not be weary in well doing: for in due season we shall reap, if we faint not."
Galatians 6:9

♛

Sometimes we can grow discouraged when we don't know how well we're doing. You may be an excellent mom, a great wife, an awesome leader in your local church, and yet no one is saying anything. Maybe you have embarked on uncharted waters, and are doing something that has never been done before in your family or your community. Knowing you are doing a good job can give you the extra boost that you need to continue. Don't be discouraged. Don't be weary in well doing. Don't be deflated. You are doing a great job! Keep up the good work! Keep serving as unto the Lord! Knowing your promotion and increase comes from Him. If no one else tells you, and if no one else notices, know that God sees and in due season you will reap. Your labor of love is not in vain. So no more questioning, "Am I doing this right?" "Why continue?" "Maybe what I'm doing doesn't matter." God is saying today, "Continue. What you're doing matters to Me. Keep serving as unto Me. In due season you will reap if you don't give up."

Prayer: *Father, thank You for encouraging me. I love You and choose to serve as unto You. Help keep my heart right and keep my mind focused on You. I know my reward and promotion comes from You. In Jesus' name, Amen.*

(Read Psalm 75:6)

In His Presence, We Are Restored

"So I have looked for You in the sanctuary, to see Your power and Your glory. Because Your loving kindness is better than life, my lips shall praise You. Thus I will bless you You while I live; I will lift up my hands in Your name" Psalm 63; 2-4, NKJV.

As we seek our Father in Heaven daily, we are shown new depths of His love. From my personal experience, His compassion goes far beyond anything I have ever witnessed or imagined.

Are you feeling unloved? Are you feeling unworthy? Are you feeling like you just don't have the strength or will to go through one more day? Do you feel drained and that if one more situation comes up you are just going to explode? Do you feel your journey is at a stand still and things are never going to be better or change? Do feel like the light at the end of your tunnel has grown dim, even as a Christian?

Well, I have some good news for you today. I want you to stop whatever you're doing for five minutes and find a quiet place, even if it is in the bathroom. Close your eyes and imagine yourself at the precious feet of Jesus. Say, "Lord, I come to You just as I am. You know what I am feeling and what I have been going through. I am sorry I have not come to You sooner but I am here now and realize Your timing is perfect. I desperately need You to restore me with Your supernatural power. I come in faith and believe You will help me right now in Jesus name. I love You and thank you for doing in me what I could never do on my own."

I want you to know how priceless you are to our Lord and Savior. He cares for you at all times. Through all the good and bad He remains faithful. In His presence, we truly are restored.

Prayer: *Oh my faithful God. I thank You for being so good to me. I thank You for restoring me and renewing me for Your name's sake and for Your glory. In Jesus name I pray, Amen.*

A Spirit of Wisdom

"[For I always pray to] the God of our Lord Jesus Christ, the Father of glory, that He may grant you a spirit of wisdom and revelation [of insight into mysteries and secrets] in the [deep and intimate] knowledge of Him" Ephesians 1:17, Amplified.

It is what we consistently do that shows a spirit's control in our lives. If you lie once, the enemy tempted you and you fell into his trap once, prayerfully never to fall into that same trap again. But to lie on a regular basis indicates a spirit of lying and deceit that has taken control. This is the enemy's goal and this is when deliverance is needed in order for us to be free.

God wants our lives to be governed by Him, to where we're not only operating in wisdom once, but in every situation. What an awesome blessing!

Our Father is saying to us today, "I want you, as My daughter, to have a spirit of wisdom and revelation. I want to show you great and mighty things you never knew. I want to show you a new side of Me and make you rich in experiences with My love and grace. I want to reveal My secrets to you. My divine plan. With everything that is going on in the world today, you must not formulate opinions and conclusions based on what you see or hear. You need insight that only comes from Me. Seek Me with all your heart and you'll find Me, ready to download My wisdom into your heart that will bring you honor and glory."

Prayer: *Father God, thank You. I need a spirit of wisdom and revelation in the knowledge of You. I submit to You and choose to walk in what You would have me to do. I thank You for delivering me from the control of the enemy and for taking complete control of my life. In Jesus' name, Amen.*

(See Ephesians 1:16-19; 1 Corinthians 1:30; James 1:5)

Divine Friendships

"As iron sharpens iron, so a man sharpens the countenance of his friend" Proverbs 27:17, NKJV

⚜

A divine friendship is a relationship that God forms between two people, of which He is at the center. As long as God is at the core of it, it continues to be divine. These relationships are edifying and enriching, and are a tremendous blessing from the Lord.

Divine friendships challenge your spiritual growth, allows you freedom to be yourself, pushes you towards fulfilling Your purpose, and improves the overall quality of your life. However, sometimes even the most divine friendships can hurt and disappoint you, because we are all subject to make mistakes. When this happens, remember to keep small matters small, and always pray about the right time and the right way to express your heart.

If God was the One that formed it, He must remain in the center of it. Rather than spending so much time chatting about life, marriage and the kids, be sure to devote some time together in heartfelt prayer and in the Word of God. This will help strengthen the friendship and will protect it from the tricks of the enemy.

Together, decide a day and time to discuss these verses of scripture on friendship with your closest friends. Share what these Scriptures mean to you: Proverbs 17:17; Proverbs 27:17; Ecclesiastes 4:9-12

Prayer: *Father God, I pray You bless me with a divine friendship. I pray that You will stay at the center of it and strengthen it with Your love. In Jesus' Name, Amen.*

The Lord Will Get You There

"I had fainted, unless I had believed to see the goodness of the LORD in the land of the living."
Psalm 27:13

If your faith has brought you this far, it is your faith that will carry you on to the other side of glory! You may have come through the fire and through the flood, and you may have thought, "I don't know how I'm going to reach that place God has for me!" But God says, "Behold I have opened a door before you and no man can shut it. For you have a little strength. You have kept my word and have not denied my name. (see Revelation 3:8)"

If He can bring you through the pain and suffering, He can usher you into the land of the living. Don't lose confidence in your Lord. Don't limit His wisdom and grace. God will be glorified in your life! As you continue walking with Him, you will see His salvation and His glory manifested in your life!

Prayer: *Thank You God. You know exactly where I am. You are my God and I am Your daughter. You gave me a heart to believe and it is that believing that is keeping me. Thank You for never letting me go. Thank You for Your mercy and grace. Thank You for loving me the way You do. I believe in You. I trust You. Be glorified in me. In Jesus name, Amen.*

(Read Psalm 37:23-37)

From God's Heart to His Daughter

"For the LORD comforts Zion; he comforts all her waste places and makes her wilderness like Eden, her desert like the garden of the LORD; joy and gladness will be found in her, thanksgiving and the voice of song" Isaiah 51:3, ESV.

Take a moment and let every word of this verse become your own.

For the LORD comforts me; He comforts all my waste places and makes my wilderness like Eden, my desert like the garden of the LORD; joy and gladness will be found in me, thanksgiving and the voice of song.

These words are from God's heart to encourage and strengthen you. If you only knew the depth of His love. If you only knew how much He cares about every detail of your life. He has not left your side. He has not left you comfortless and without hope. He will comfort your waste places. Every area that you may have wanted to give up on because it seemed hopeless, He will enrich and minister healing. Those dry and barren places in your life, He will cause them to flourish. He will turn your sadness into joy and gladness. You will see just how good your God is, and you will sing.

All of this, because you are His daughter, and there's nothing you can do to change how He feels about you.

Prayer: *Hallelujah. Father God, I praise You. I receive Your words to my heart. I receive Your love. It touches me to know that You love me more than anything. It's overwhelming. I love You, and even though I don't understand why You love me so much, I receive it. Love me. Bless me. Enrich me. Comfort me. Heal me. Cause my life to bring You great glory. In Jesus name, Amen.*

Come closer.

"Come close to God, and God will come close to you. Wash your hands, you sinners; purify your hearts, for your loyalty is divided between God and the world" James 4:8, NLT.

When my husband and I are sitting on a sofa, and he is on one end and I'm on the other, I sometimes look at him and say, "Come over here. You feel distant." And then there are times when I'm not talking or opening up to him. He'll look at me and say, "Hey, what's on your mind? You feel distant." We as humans long to feel close to those we love, allowing nothing to come between us.

Maybe you are on the opposite of the couch in your heart and God is on the other. You want one thing, and He wants the other. Maybe you are not opening up to Him in prayer. Maybe everything feels confusing in your life right now, and you have no words.

It's not God that is distant. It's you.

God is saying, "Come closer to Me. You feel distant. I can help you. I can be everything you need. This is not the time to distance yourself from me. Draw near and receive My peace, my comfort, my grace and my love. I won't turn you away."

Prayer: *Father God, I thank you for speaking to me. I am sorry for distancing myself from you. I come close right now, and I ask that you come close to me. I need you like never before. Wrap your arms around me and let me feel your presence. Touch my heart and my mind. Strengthen me, God. Help me to abide in you. In Jesus name, Amen.*

(Read James 4:7-8)

A Need to Please

*"Every good gift and every perfect gift is from above,
and cometh down from the Father of lights, with
whom is no variableness, neither shadow of turning"*
James 1:17, KJV.

꙳

So many of us go throughout our entire life trying hard to make others happy, feeling a need to please, and never wanting to disappoint those we love. The reward may be their smile and gratitude, but the consequence is pure exhaustion.

When God divinely places someone in your life, you don't have to try so hard. If you never called to pray with them, they would still love you. If you never invited them over for dinner, they would still love you. More than what you do, they sincerely love YOU. You have found favor in their eyes and it's not based on what you do or don't do.

God is the same way. Don't try to

work so hard to win the affection of a loving God that is already fully convinced of His love for you. Ease up on yourself dear and begin to enjoy the Lord, enjoy your life, and enjoy the relational treasures He has given you. They are rich blessings designed to enrich your life, not add sorrow to it.

Prayer: *Father God, forgive me if I have frustrated Your grace. When I try hard to make others happy, I end up exhausted. Thank You for reminding me of Your love and grace. Keep me secure in Your love and enjoying the life and the people You have given me. In Jesus Name, Amen.*

Don't Go There

"Be not overcome of evil, but overcome evil with good" Romans 12:21, KJV.

Some people are like kids on an elevator; they will push every emotional button on you, never realizing they are being used by the enemy. When everything in you wants to react in a negative way, don't go there. Remember, whoever overcomes you controls you (see 2 Peter 2:19).

Your determination to consistently show kindness and love are too much for anyone to handle. Good will always win over evil. Many times I have cried in my time alone with God because I didn't want to be the bigger person. I didn't want to walk in love or do the right thing. Oh, but thank God for His supernatural help! It is only by His divine grace and power that we can do anything good.

When we learn to submit to God, we

find that He makes it easier to love the unlovable.

He reminds us of the influence we have. Somebody, even if it's one person, is watching you, your responses and your example. Walk in love while you continue to live the life God has blessed you to live, moving forward in doing what God has purposed you to do. My sister, don't go there!

Prayer: *Father God, I thank You for the help of Your Holy Spirit. You loved me enough to put Your Spirit within me to help me. When everything in me wants to behave ugly, help me Lord to stay in love and not go there. I rebuke all strife and wrath in my heart, and I yield to You Lord. Be glorified in me. In Jesus' Name, Amen.*

Seek Him, See Him and Be Changed

"And ye shall seek me, and find me, when ye shall search for me with all your heart. And I will be found of you, saith The Lord..."
Jeremiah 29:13-14a, KJV

༺

When you seek God with all of your heart, you will see Him. When you search for Him, you find Him. No one who has a real encounter with God remains the same. When you are desperate to see a change in your life and desperate to be free of that issue you've dealt with for far too long, only then do you seek God with all of your heart. At the heart of wholehearted seeking is a cry that says, "Lord, if You don't do this, it can't be done." God promises when you seek Him with that kind of reckless abandonment, you will find Him. You will see a different side of Him, a different side of His love that you've never seen before, and you will experience change. "I will be found by you," He promises.

Anytime a negative mind, a cold heart, or a lost soul has a beautiful and real encounter with God; they are never the same. When you want to see your husband change, pray for God to bless him with a real encounter with His love. When you want your enemies to stop being so cruel and hateful toward you, pray for God to bless them with a real encounter with Himself. God loves to answer that prayer!

That life-changing moment isn't always dramatic like that of Paul on the road to Damascus but often occurs through our experiences with His sons and daughters. We are someone's encounter with the love of God, with His power and with His peace. Seek Him with desperation, and you will see Him, and when you see Him you will be changed into the same image, from glory to glory, and will be used to bless others.

Prayer: *Father, thank You for Your word to me. I*

receive it. I am desperate for You, desperate to see you in my life, so I seek You to discover a new side of You. In Jesus' name, Amen.

Hello Princess

*"Behold, I give unto you power to tread on serpents
and scorpions, and over all the power of the enemy:
and nothing shall by any means hurt you.
Notwithstanding in this rejoice not, that the spirits
are subject unto you; but rather rejoice, because your
names are written in heaven"*
Luke 10:19-20, KJV.

♛

Recently while speaking to a group of incarcerated women, I discovered that many of them were struggling with their identity in Christ. But it's a common problem for women everywhere. Many of us struggle with who we are and what we have to offer. The world has done a good job of setting values on people and things—and many times we feel like we just don't measure up. For instance, when you hear the word "princess," you more than likely picture a beautiful woman in a ball gown wearing jewels. One person I am sure you did not picture in your mind is YOU.

A princess is a daughter of a king who has been given the rights and privileges of a kingdom. You, my sister, are a daughter of the King, a princess, given all the rights and privileges of the Kingdom of God. Jesus has given us the power, authority, control, and mastery over the enemy. Because of this power, we are able to trample over all the force and strength of the enemy. The authority to be victorious over every life situation has been given to us, Princess, by our King, Jesus. We are operating under HIS authority and in HIS strength.

Living the life of a princess who operates in her rights and privileges of the Kingdom of God brings glory to Him. A princess knows who she is, knows and operates in her authority, and ultimately rejoices that her precious name is written in heaven!

So, when we look at ourselves in the mirror, we say, "Hello, Princess who walks in victory over the enemy and whose name is written in heaven. Have a glorious day walking in the strength of our KING, JESUS! Amen."

Prayer: *Dear Heavenly Father, I first thank You that my name is written in heaven. I thank You that I am a princess and I will walk in the authority given to me by King Jesus. I ask that You help me to see myself as a princess, especially when times are tough and things look bad. I ask that You help me to not be moved by the way things look and only be moved by my faith in Your word. In Jesus' Name I pray. Amen.*

A Better Way to Live

"Come to Me, all you who labor and are heavy-laden and overburdened, and I will cause you to rest. [I will ease and relieve and refresh your souls.]Take My yoke upon you and learn of Me, for I am gentle (meek) and humble (lowly) in heart, and you will find rest (relief and ease and refreshment and recreation and blessed quiet) for your souls."
Matthew 11:28-29, Amplified

Early one morning, I decided to make a quick run to the grocery store. I ran inside and picked up one of the baskets near the front entrance and began to shop. As I placed different items into the basket, I began to notice it getting heavier. I then picked up a large gallon of milk and glanced at the basket, wondering, "How am I going to carry this heavy load?" Just as I was about to figure out a way, a gentleman stopped me. He said, "You know ma'am, you don't have to carry that basket like that." I didn't understand what he was saying until he walked over, pulled a lever from the side of my basket and suddenly transformed it into something that rolled on the floor! I laughed and thanked him for showing me a better way.

So many of us are walking through life carrying heavy loads God never intended for us to take on. Just when we figure out how to carry one burden, we add another one on top of it. We think to ourselves, "Lord, how am I going to bear all of these heavy loads?" Whatever it may be, God will do for you, through Christ, the same thing that nice gentleman did for me in that grocery store—He will show you a better way. Let Him lift every burden that weighs you down and give you His wisdom and instructions that are light. Allow Jesus the opportunity to step in, transform your life and show you a better way to live!

Prayer: *My Lord, thank You for speaking to me. Help me Lord. Transform my life and show me a better way to live. In Jesus Name, Amen.*

You Are Blessed!

"So don't be afraid, little flock. For it gives your Father great happiness to give you the Kingdom"
Luke 12:32, NLT.

♛

Settle this within yourself this morning of how tremendously blessed you are. It's not when you get the desires of your heart that you will become blessed. No, you are blessed right now! Discontentment can tell you that you need this or that before you can truly be happy. Only to find that when you finally obtain the things you want, you are now on to the next thing. Never satisfied.

The people of Israel wandered in the desert for forty years, looking to reach the land that God had promised. Their hearts were full of complaints and murmuring. They were frustrated with God, with their situation, upset with Moses, and at each others' throats because they couldn't see how blessed they were. Although living in tents isn't the Ritz, living in God is. They had forgotten their rich heritage and the mighty God they served.

It's insulting to God when we don't see how blessed we are already. If you know the King of kings and the Lord of lords, and if you are a daughter of the King, then sister girl, you are truly blessed!

Prayer: *Father, You are good to me. Thank You for all that You have done. Help me to walk throughout this day with a thankful heart. I have nothing to complain about and no reason to murmur. I could be dead, but I'm alive. I could be lost, but I'm found in You. Having a relationship with You means more than any material blessing. I'm Your daughter, and You are my God, and I'm content with that. In Jesus' Name, Amen.*

You don't have to hurt anymore.

"The Spirit of the Sovereign LORD is on me, because the LORD has anointed me to proclaim good news to the poor. He has sent me to bind up the brokenhearted, to proclaim freedom for the captives and release from darkness for the prisoners"
Isaiah 61:1, NIV.

People with broken hearts will hurt you before you hurt them. They will reject you before you reject them. They will leave you before you leave them, all in an attempt to protect their hearts from experiencing more pain. Their unspoken cry is, "Please don't take it personally, I'm just hurting and I'm afraid," but seldom will they admit it. I'm so glad God comes after us in our broken state. He's not afraid of us hurting Him. He's not intimidated.

I'm so thankful He heals our hearts as

He removes our hand from our chest, revealing how bad the wound really is. Then He stitches up our hearts, fills us with His love, reassures us that we're going to be ok and then sends us to out to minister healing to others. You can be healed. You can be free to give and receive love. You don't have to be a victim. You can be victorious through Jesus. You don't have to hurt anymore. You can be free today.

Prayer: *Father God I need healing in my heart. Touch me Lord with your hand and make me new, whole and complete in you. Fill me with your love and give me the strength to help others just like me. In Jesus name, Amen.*

It Takes Courage

ᨃ

It takes courage
to tell the truth
to follow your heart
to do something alone
to make yourself vulnerable
to leave a longtime love
to trust again
to speak up
to wait on God's best
to start something new
to admit your own ignorance
to believe things will change
to give expecting nothing in return
to be yourself

Often we find God saying throughout Scripture, "Be strong and courageous." "Take heart." "Take courage." While negative situations come to deflate and discourage us, God gives us the necessary ingredient to face life's challenges head on-courage. Often it is our most shortest prayers that are most successful with the Lord. We always will receive an immediate response to, "Lord, help me." Even though you don't express specifically what you need help with, He already knows. His help is like an ocean poured into a small cup without wasting a drop. He loves you that much.

Let God give you the courage you need in order to do what you never thought you could do. Let Him give you the courage to succeed pass your limitations, to face tomorrow, to enjoy life today, to face your fears, to change your world, to face your inner critic, and to embrace the truth of who you are in Him.

Prayer: *Thank You Father. Fill me with Your Holy Spirit and help me do what I have been so afraid to do. I know You have not given me a spirit of fear, but of power and of love and a sound mind. Help me understand what that means for me. In Jesus Name.*

(Read 2 Timothy 1:7)

He is Your Everything

"Whom have I in heaven but you? And earth has nothing I desire besides you." Psalm 73:25

"I say to the LORD, "You are my God." Hear, LORD, my cry for mercy." Psalm 140:6

"I say to the LORD, "You are my Lord; apart from you I have no good thing." Psalm 16:2 NIV

♔

There is no person who can fulfill your life, your heart, as your God can. He takes the place of every relationship in your life and serves as your everything. Anything that brings you earthly happiness can be replaced with Him, but there is no single person or thing on this earth that can give you the joy that only He has to offer.

Whatever you may be lacking in your life today, whether that be a friend, a father, a man, know that God Himself is enough for you. I remember once begging God for relationships in my life and Him speaking to my spirit, "Daughter, until you realize I am all you truly need, you will never be satisfied." He wants you to depend on Him. Rely on Him. Trust Him. Know He is your everything. Before He places something magnificent in your hands, they must be empty, first. Rid yourself of the idea that you need anything aside from Him in your life today. Because sister, there is no other friend, no father, no love like that of the One who loved you, first (1 John 4:19).

He is your Shepherd who keeps watch over you (Ezekiel 34:11-16) (Psalm 121:3). He is your Friend who loves you at all times (Proverbs 17:17). He is your Father who calls you His own (1 John 3:10). And He is Your first love (Revelation 2:4).

Prayer: *Father, I know that you are my everything, and I praise your worthy name. Forgive me for thinking any other person could satisfy my soul as only you can. Fill me, Lord, and show up for me this very day. I love you, and my heart beats for you,*

Jesus. You are mine, and I am yours. In your precious name, Amen.

(Read Psalms 107:9; Psalms 119:57; Isaiah 40:28-31)

God hears your cry.

"And if (since) we [positively] know that He listens to us in whatever we ask, we also know [with settled and absolute knowledge] that we have [granted us as our present possessions] the requests made of Him"
1 John 5:15, AMP.

I returned home one night and didn't have the door key. Needless to say, my husband whom I love was inside sleeping like a rock. He didn't hear me knocking on the door like the police. He didn't hear me ringing the doorbell repeatedly. He didn't hear me throw a bucket next to the window. That man was completely out. So I yelled to our bedroom window, "Baby, open the door!" A minute later there he was standing at the front door. I asked him, "You didn't hear all of the noise I was making?" He said, "No". I asked him, "What woke you up?" He said, "I heard your voice."

Maybe you're like me, you're making a

lot of noise trying to get God's attention. Maybe you're wondering why He's not answering you and why He hasn't changed your situation.

But always remember God hears your voice. He knows what you're going through and He cares about every detail of your life. He can and will open great doors for you that have seemed impossible. He will open doors in His timing and in His own creative way. He will respond to your voice and to your trust in Him.

Prayer: *Father God, I thank you that you hear me when I pray. And if I know you hear me, I know I have what I am requesting of you. In Jesus name, Amen.*

A Special Prayer for You

꒰ꉂ꒱

Father God, I pray for Your daughter who is reading this right now. You love her deeply and there is nothing she can do to make You stop loving her. I thank You for Your precious blood that covers her and her loved ones. Thank You for Your Holy Spirit that fills her. Thank You for Your Word that instructs her and helps her grow. You are a wonderful God and You care about every detail of her life. Bless her Lord. You've brought her a long way. Bless her and let her know everything is going to be alright. You see her pain, her struggles and You've heard her prayers. Grace her to run her race. Propel her forward, Father. Help her to move forward and walk by faith and not by what they see. No matter what her feelings are at the moment and no matter what the devil is saying, all that matters is what You've said about her. Help her to trust in You like she's never trusted in You before. I pray You take Your place on the throne of her heart. Help her take her place as being seated in heavenly places in Christ Jesus, and help her keep the enemy under her feet as she walks in the authority You have given her through Jesus. She is victorious through Christ even when she don't feel victorious. Help her combat every lie of the enemy with the truth of Your Word. And when life seems overwhelming, help her remember to steal away to be strengthened by You. Your grace is enough for her. Help her release every person and every situation to You that's been weighing so heavy on her heart and calm every fear with Your love. Flood her with supernatural peace and bring quietness to her soul. In Jesus' name I pray, Amen.

(Read Jeremiah 33:3; 2 Corinthians 12:9)

Be Steadfast, Unmovable, Always Abounding

"So, my dear brothers and sisters, be strong and immovable. Always work enthusiastically for the Lord, for you know that nothing you do for the Lord is ever useless" 1 Corinthians 15:58, NLT.

♔

The enemy may be telling you, "Why continue? You might as well hang it up and do something else." Whether you are a minister, a missionary, a school teacher, a volunteer, a caretaker, etc, know that your labor is not in vain. You are making a difference whether you see visible change or not.

The Bible instructs us to be steadfast, unmovable, always abounding in the work God has given us to do. Know that your labor is not in vain. You may not see any visible proof of the difference God is using you to make, but you are making a difference. Don't be moved. Don't lose heart. Don't lose your eternal perspective. Continue to abound in His work and He will cause all of grace and favor to abound toward you.

Prayer: *Father God, I thank You for speaking directly to my heart. Only You know how I truly feel. I repent for every time I've complained about the assignment You've given me. I receive Your supernatural encouragement and Your touch. Thank You for giving me the victory through Jesus. No matter how it looks. No matter how I feel. No matter what I hear. Help me to persevere and endure. Restore my soul and my passion for the work You've called me to. Help me to maintain my joy and an eternal perspective. Help me stay excited and not listen to the lies of the enemy. Thank You that I get to glorify You by making a difference in someone's life. In the name of Jesus, Amen.*

(Read 1 Corinthians 15:57,58)

Reasons for the Storms

"For our light affliction, which is but for a moment, worketh for us a far more exceeding and eternal weight of glory" 2 Corinthians 4:17.

You are a living epistle read by men and God's light shines through you. If you think people are watching you now, wait until you face a difficult season in your life. The eyes of anyone within your sphere of influence will zero in wanting to see how you will respond and if you will do what you have preached all those years to them. They want to see if you will forgive those that hurt you, if you will still believe God after you have been diagnosed, if you will still serve God with passion after you've lost someone you love, and if you will continue to walk with God even though you don't understand why it happened to you.

This is not to sound insensitive to your pain that you may have experienced.

Nor is this to infer that God did this horrible thing to you to win someone to Jesus. No, absolutely not! God is not to blame. He does however allow trials for reasons that only He knows. Could it be that your trust and reliance upon Him in the midst of adversity is just what those around you need to see in order to know that God is real?

We pray for God to save those we love, yet we do not know how He will do it. Yet, God in His infinite wisdom will allow a storm in our lives knowing that He is going to be glorified in it. Is the storm then worth it? Yes, you better believe it is! God knows that your faith in Him and your resilience in the storm will do more in reaching your loved ones than anything you could ever say.

Be willing then to go through the storm and face the adversity head on if it means the eternal salvation of those you love! It works for you a far more exceeding and eternal weight of glory!

Prayer: *Father, I hear You. Thank You for Your*

comfort and for giving me understanding. In every trial I face, I count it all joy knowing that You have a greater work that You are accomplishing. I am willing to go through the storm if it means that those around me will see Your light in me and come to know You for themselves. Be glorified in my life! In Jesus name, Amen.

(Read 2 Corinthians 4; 2 Corinthians 3:2; James 1:2)

Persevere Through the Bad and the Good

"Consider it pure joy, my brothers and sisters, whenever you face trials of many kinds, because you know that the testing of your faith produces perseverance. Let perseverance finish its work so that you may be mature and complete, not lacking anything." James 1:2-4

How sweet it is to commune with God, to feel His love, learn His wisdom and experience His power. It is wonderful! Just when you find yourself enjoying a state of peace from your communion with God, the enemy sends a trial that is difficult, emotionally challenging and that tests everything you know to be true.

In these moments it can be difficult to understand how and why your circumstances have changed so drastically.

But understand this, everything you go through is working for your good and for the glory of God. You may say, "Well, how can this horrible situation be working for my good? How can my husband leaving me and our kids be for my good? How can suffering financial ruin be for my good?" These are the questions of the heart that only God's word provides answer for. What does God's word say? "The Lord is good and His mercy endures forever!" God is good even when people and situations aren't.

You may be experiencing everything bad, but trust in the goodness of God. Let Him produce in you a persevering heart. Let Him complete the work He began in you. Every lesson learned brings you a step closer to Him. He will allow you to come across difficult people so that you may learn His love, His compassion and forgiveness. He may remove something from your life to help you realize that all you need is Him. He may bring you up against seemingly impossible challenges so you will finally know and believe that you can do all things through Christ. We all have times when we think, "Why do I have to face this God? Everything was going so well!" And then He remind us that He has a purpose for everything we face. You would not be the woman you are today had you not faced some painful situations that helped developed your character and that showed you God is indeed present in your life.

Prayer: *Dear Heavenly Father, I thank You for giving me the strength to face whatever may come my way. I ask that You renew my mind so whenever I face a new challenge, I remain in peace knowing that You have allowed it to develop me and bring glory to Your name. Help me trust in Your goodness. I love You and I receive Your love and grace. In Jesus name, Amen.*

It's In The Waiting

"I waited patiently for the Lord; he turned to me and heard my cry." Psalm 40:1 NIV

One morning I went to chapel at my son's university. I had been sick and recovering for four years from cancer and unable to step into the house of the Lord. It is was a precious privilege to step into His sanctuary and participate in corporate worship. They began to sing, "Everlasting God." "Strength arise as we wait upon the Lord, as we wait upon the Lord..." and God began to give me a renewed revelation about waiting.

I prayed every day and a multitude of times for my healing, but healing did not manifest as quickly as I hoped. I have been waiting for restoration, waiting to get back to ministry and waiting and waiting and still waiting. Have you ever been in a place in your life where God instructs you to wait? It can be hard to wait. In our fast paced society that does not like to wait for anything, we don't like waiting in fast food lines. We roll through stop signs. We don't even like to wait for people to finish talking before we speak or leave a message. We've become a culture that has lost the value of the 4th fruit of the spirit, "patience." We want something to do to fill in the time, but God says, "Wait My daughter."

With tears streaming down my face, I realized I could wait, needed to and wanted to wait for whatever God wants to do next in my life.

There are times in the Bible, God tells us to wait. Jesus tells His disciples to go to Jerusalem and wait for the gift His Father promised. The disciples knew nothing of the Holy Spirit and had no idea what they were waiting for. Romans 8:19 says, "The creation waits in eager expectation for the sons (and daughters) of God to be revealed." And I Thess. 1:10 tells us "we are to wait for his Son from heaven."

God is doing something on the inside of us that yet cannot be put into words. We don't need to know how long; we just need to be obedient and wait. We need to wait patiently, with eager expectation for Jesus Christ to reveal himself to us for blessed are all who wait for Him.

Prayer: *Thank you Lord for the strength and patience to wait. I wait patiently with eager expectation for what you desire for me. Help me to be strong and take heart in Jesus Name, Amen.*

Yet I Will Rejoice

"Though the fig tree does not bud and there are no grapes on the vines, though the olive crop fails and the fields produce no food, though there are no sheep in the pen and no cattle in the stalls, yet I will rejoice in the Lord, I will be joyful in God my Savior"
Habakkuk 3:17-18, NIV

♔

Habakkuk wondered why God was allowing such suffering for his people. Why would the Lord punish something evil (the Assyrians) with something just as evil (the Babylonians), while allowing His people (the Hebrews) to continue to suffer, be invaded, and be exiled?

God answered that all that was going on—world empires rising and falling—is in His hands. Though it seems that the wicked triumph, in the end God and His righteousness will win and He will keep His promises to His people.

Like Habakkuk, we wonder and

question. We don't understand what God is doing in the suffering on the other side of the planet or the suffering that invades our own hearts and lives. But the end has already been determined. God wins; good wins. "For the earth will be filled with the knowledge of the glory of the Lord, as the waters cover the sea" (Habakkuk 2:14).

That's what we hang our hats on. At the end of the day when nothing makes sense to our little minds, when all we do seems a tiny drop of good in an ocean of evil—we know that God will one day make everything right.

Habakkuk was privileged to receive a vision of God's power over two world empires. Years would pass beyond his lifetime, but God's promise would come true. Habakkuk trusted even when what was right in front of him made no sense-crops dead, flocks gone, economy collapsing. He could rejoice in God because ultimately that is where joy must remain focused. No matter how bad circumstances may be "the Sovereign Lord is my strength; he makes my feet like the feet of a deer, he enables me to tread on the heights" (Habakkuk3:19).

I heard an illustration once of a speaker mentioning a conversation with a friend who said she was doing okay "under the circumstances." The speaker asked her the question, "What are you doing under your circumstances?"

Commit yourself to walk "above" your circumstances with joy in your heart enabled by the strength of your sovereign Lord and the promise of His ultimate victory. Put on joy and strength from the Lord and rise above whatever difficult circumstances have invaded your life. Then watch what God will do.

Prayer: *Thank You for the blessing of a new year, Lord. In this year, no matter what happens, "yet I will rejoice" because I trust You to work Your will. Help me to be "above" my circumstances because I trust in You, the One who is above all.*

Peace Check

*"Therefore I say to you, do not worry about your life,
what you will eat or what you will drink; nor about
your body, what you will put on. Is not life more
than food and the body more than clothing?"*
Matthew 6:25

Webster's Dictionary defines peace as "an agreement or treaty to end hostilities." If we are to experience peace in our daily lives, what are the "hostilities" that need to be reckoned with? Most of the time, peace ceases when concern becomes anxiety.

Concern stems from a caring feeling about someone or something, and allows God to be involved. Anxiety, however, is a tormenting form of worry that focuses on the problem instead of on God. To protect our peace, we must learn to thwart anxiety before it begins. There are three ways to recognize the onset of anxiety:

- If you find that you are more

concerned with what YOU desire rather than the will of God, you are heading for a period of anxiety.

- If you find yourself feeling hurried into making unwise decisions, you are inviting anxiety.
- If you are living in a constant state of agitation and uneasiness, you are likely suppressing anxious feelings.

Walking in peace does not involve escaping reality or responsibility; rather, peace enables us to face trials and hardships with genuine confidence in God. Peace guards our hearts and minds from damaging thoughts.

Use your quiet time today to conduct a "peace check." Examine your spirit in the presence of the Lord and commit to banish anxious feelings when they arise.

Prayer: *Lord, examine my heart to see if I am resisting Your divine peace by focusing on what I want, making unwise and hurried decisions, or experiencing agitation.*

God is Speaking

"Then I heard the voice of the Lord, saying "Whom will I send? Who will go for us?" I said, "Here I am. Send me!" Isaiah 6:8

God is always speaking but only a few are ever listening. Silence in the spiritual realm isn't the result of God's distance but ours. God is forever asking, forever sending, and forever saving, but only those who are interested in His presence and listening for His voice will ever know it. In this case, Isaiah wasn't "called"-he was listening when God was calling anyone who would listen. Isaiah had his mind and ears on God and was ready and willing to do whatever needed to be done.

He was not waiting for a specific call; he was just waiting for God to speak. God spoke and Isaiah answered: "Here I am. Send me!" (Isaiah 6:8). Were there others who could have answered? Probably, but

Isaiah didn't hesitate to answer, and because of that, events in his life were set into motion that changed the course of history.

THERE ARE NO ACCIDENTS AND NO COINCIDENCES WITH GOD!

There is no such thing as "chance" or "luck." One of the most powerful ways God speaks to us is through the things that happen in our life, especially those things that are totally out of our control. God is speaking to us all the time through the events in our life and we need to realize that what happens to us is happening for a reason. We may never fully understand or comprehend that reason, but nothing happens in our life that God doesn't allow.

Hearing from God is like anything else, it takes practice. If you want to hear God's voice, you have got to practice listening to God's voice. The more you practice hearing God, the more you will hear God. The first thing you will be amazed at is how much God is speaking to you. Like I said earlier, God is always speaking to you. The problem is, we are not always listening.

When God speaks to you, what He says will always be in line with His Word. God will never contradict His Word. God is not going to tell you to do something that He has told you not to do in His Word.

"If you want more of God, more guidance, and more direction, then learn His Word. Make it your goal to be alert to His voice and to stand up and say, "Here I am. Send me." - Haley DiMarco

Prayer: *Heavenly Father, It is written in Your Word according to John chapter 10 that Your sheep know Your Voice. Heavenly Father, I am one of Your sheep. I ask You to teach me to hear Your Voice distinctly and clearly. I ask that You clear my mind of any preconceived thoughts, confusion or deception. I ask You Lord to block anything that is not of You so that I can hear your voice only, Lord Jesus. I ask You Lord in complete faith and confidence that You will not allow any words to be spoken from my mouth that are not Your Words, in Jesus name I pray, Amen.*

A Special Prayer for You

༶

Father God, I take a moment to pray for Your daughter who is reading this. Lord she belongs to You and You are hers. You have called her out and have consecrated her for Your use. You have worked in and through her life and she has seen for herself that You are real. Now she has reached a place where she needs You more now than ever. Lord, I pray with everything in me that You fill every valley, every ditch and every lacking place in her. Fill her Lord with Your fullness, with Your love and with Your Spirit. Cause any mountain, any hill and any high thing that is trying to exalt itself against the knowledge of Your will to be brought low and into submission of You. Cause anything crooked and out of the way to be made straight in her. Cause any area in her heart and mind that's rough to be made smooth. Have your way in and through her. Flow in and through her. You promised Lord that out of her belly shall flow rivers of living waters. I pray those living rivers will minister health and life to her, and bring health and life to her surroundings. Be glorified in her Lord in a mighty way and make her a true testament of Your grace and love. Your Word is forever settled in heaven and I pray Your Word is forever settled in her mind and heart. May it settle every issue in her thoughts and bring supernatural peace to her now. In the name of Jesus, Amen.

(Read Luke 3:4-6; John 7:38; Psalm 119:89)

Stay By the Fire

"Sin will be rampant everywhere, and the love of many will grow cold." Matthew 24:12 , NLT.

"Come close to God, and God will come close to you. Wash your hands, you sinners; purify your hearts, for your loyalty is divided between God and the world." James 4:8, NLT

When it is cold outside we naturally turn on the heat to keep ourselves warm. We cover ourselves with blankets and gather by the fire. We do what we can to protect ourselves from being affected by the harsh climate. It is bitter cold in the world today and sin is rampant.

With the actions of many people being uncharacteristic of God, what are we doing to keep our love from growing cold? We must draw near to God and let Him draw near to us. If you don't stay close to the spiritual warmth of God's love and deepening your knowledge of Him, you will allow situation and circumstance to offend you and cause you to fall away. The colder it is in the world, the more you must run to the Fire of God's Word and receive His truth, receive His understanding and His Spirit. Let His peace flow in and through you like warm liquid. Refuse to remain offended with anyone.

Doing this will keep the enemy out and keep God's love in. You don't have to side with the world. Everyone will have their opinion of why someone is behaving the way they are, but you, let God show you the deeper meaning. In all your getting get understanding. Understanding and love are directly proportional. The more understanding you have from God about someone, the better you can relate to them.

Let God bless you with understanding so that you can love better in this day and time. Draw close to Him in love and humility and He will turn on the heat in your heart and increase your love capacity. It is cold outside. Stay by the Fire.

Prayer: *Father, thank You for speaking to me. It is cold and dark in this world. I draw near to You. Enlarge my heart and keep my love warm God. Don't let me grow cold and callous. Help me stay by the warmth of Your presence and in Your Word. Fill me with Your Holy Spirit and be glorified in me. In Jesus' name, Amen.*

What You Can Do Instead of Worrying

"Who of you by worrying can add a single hour to your life? Since you cannot do this very little thing, why do you worry about the rest?"
Luke 12:25-26, NIV.

Here, Jesus tells us that we can't accomplish anything by worrying, not even small feats. But God knows that we worry. He knows that sometimes we perceive our circumstances to be bigger than they are because we're focusing too much on our problems and not enough on Him.

What He wants us to do during these times is to trust and praise Him through it, seeking His peace and direction. He wants us to remember that we have someone on our side who could not only add an hour to our lives, but who created time itself. He wants us to continue walking the path, not worrying about what will be because He already has it all taken care of. And sometimes that takes work for us. So what can you do when you feel worry creeping up?

1. Focus on God and His love for you. Remember that He desires to see you prosper.

2. Write out situations in the past where you were worried about the outcome but you saw how God came through. Refer back to those times as reminders of His great power and presence in your life.

3. Find and memorize scripture. Hide it in your heart.

4. Pray, praise, and thank Him in the thick of it. When your praises go up, your circumstances
begin to look much smaller as you realize you have someone who's power exceeds all things.

5. Do your best, and surrender the outcome to God.

Worrying steals our ability to enjoy the moments that God has given us now. This is why Jesus tells us not to worry. What you don't know, God does. What you can't do, He can. He is your partner in this life and the next. His knowledge and presence go before you in everything. Rest in knowing that anything you may be worried about, God already has it taken care of. You will see when the time is right.

Prayer: *Father today I lay my worries at Your feet. I know that You are with me now and You have my future in the palm of Your hands. I ask that You broaden my perspective and help me to see life the way You do. I declare that with You by my side, there is nothing that can over take me. You are my strength, my shield and my portion. In Jesus name, Amen.*

A Woman of Character

"For God knew his people in advance, and he chose them to become like his Son, so that his Son would be the firstborn among many brothers and sisters."
Romans 8:29, NLT

Our destiny is to look like Jesus on the inside and to behave like Jesus on the outside. Many of us are spiritual powerhouses, can pray the house down, sing the roof off, hang off the chandeliers when we praise the Lord, and can administrate duties with a spirit of excellence. We appear like strong mighty lions, but who are we inwardly? Do we love just as loud? Forgive just as strong? Are we as obedient to God as our prayers are powerful?

These are things of the heart that matter most to God. The nuts and bolts of a woman of character is how she responds when it's time to let go, how she behaves when she doesn't get her way, how she acts when her gift and calling is ignored, and what she does when she experiences failure. Let God break off everything that doesn't look like Him. The lying has to stop. The bad attitude, no more. The laziness and procrastination, no more. The unforgiveness and resentment, that's not becoming of you. No more erotic romance novels and sexual perversion. The pride and arrogance, no ma'am. The selfishness, not you woman of God. No more making a person your idol. Time to tell fear and timidity goodbye. You can be the woman you know in your heart you were created to be.

Let God break these things off so you can develop His character. You are chosen and are predestined for a great work that will bring God great glory, but His work in you is where it all begins.

Prayer: *Yes, Lord. I know whatever You reveal to me that needs changing in my life, You will help change it. You are with me. In Jesus name, Amen.*

(Read Proverbs 31:30-31; 2 Peter 1:4-8)

The Pity Party is Over

"We are troubled on every side, yet not distressed; we are perplexed, but not in despair; persecuted, but not forsaken; cast down, but not destroyed."
2 Corinthians 4:8-9

⚜

For every pity party invite you might've sent out, go and get it back and say, *"I'm not throwing a pity party today! I'm an overcomer through Jesus! I may be facing some challenges, but God's going to see me through it. I'm not going to be distressed, depressed, perplexed or in despair! My God is with me and is greater than anything I'm facing right now!"*

Focus on your God, not on your problems. He is bigger! You may be troubled on every side, but God will provide a way out for you. You may be suffering persecution, but God is with you. You may be cast down, but you are not destroyed. If you are still breathing, God has a plan to turn what the enemy has meant for your bad around for your good. God is determined to be glorified in your life! He wants people to see how you face your challenges and say, "Wow! You must know something I don't." To which you can gladly respond, "No, I know Someone! Let me introduce Him to you."

Prayer: *Father, I thank You that You are with me. You are my God and I'm yours. Through every challenge I face, Your hand will guide me. You are my shelter, my rock and my confidence. I love You Lord. I refuse to throw a pity party when You have been so good to me. Let my faith bring glory to Your name. Be glorified in me. In Jesus name, Amen.*

There will be trouble.

"Therefore, my beloved brethren, be steadfast, immovable, always abounding in the work of the Lord, knowing that your labor is not in vain in the Lord." 1 Corinthians 15:58

When you make a decision to do what God has put in your heart to do expect trouble. The enemy will stir up trouble to get your eyes off of God. Before you know it, you're emotionally stirred up because you didn't see it coming. Sometimes it can be the people closest to you that can allow themselves to be influenced by the devil to discourage you. "Be steadfast" God says, "unmovable and always abounding in the work of the Lord".

It doesn't matter who comes against you. It doesn't matter what is said about you. No one can stop the work that God has purposed and preordained beforehand for you to do. No one can knock you off your stance when your feet are planted in

God's word. Fill up your heart with the Word of God. Let it keep you. Let it preserve you. Let it remind you of who you are in Christ. Let it fight for you. "Is not my word like as unto a fire? And like a hammer that breaks the rock into pieces." What God has said, that's what will be.

It may feel like your obedience to God has caused an all out spiritual war, but don't worry. That's an indicator that you're right on track. If the devil is angry, you're doing something right. Wipe those tears from your eyes. Hold up your head and watch God move on your behalf. Even if He has to speak to someone in an audible voice to leave you alone, He will do just that. Be encouraged. Be encouraged. Be encouraged.

Prayer: *Father God, my decision to obey You has caused a war. Keep my blood pressure down. Keep my mind sound. Keep my hands to the plow. Keep my heart fixed on You. I believe Your word and I stand on Your promises. Help me to do what You have purposed beforehand for me to do. Help me plant my feet in Your word and be unmovable. No matter what trouble comes my way, I trust in You Lord. Be glorified in me. In Jesus name, Amen.*

(Read Jeremiah 23:28-29, 2 Timothy 1:9)

You can do all things.

"I can do all things through Christ which strengthens me." Philippians 4:13

Take this Scripture literally. They aren't just words on a page, they are true. Slow down and read each word carefully. I...can...do...all...things... This means with the help of God there is nothing you can't do. You can love through Christ which strengthens you. You can forgive through Christ which strengthens you. You can raise your children by yourself through Christ which strengthens you. You can be the wife God wants you to be through Christ which strengthens you. You can get your degree through Christ which strengthens you. You can fulfill your purpose through Christ which strengthens you. You can do anything you set your mind to through Christ which strengthens you.

It is in Him that you live, move and

have your being. Sometimes the people in our life make us feel so strong. They make us feel as though we can conquer the world. Maybe that person was your mother, your grandmother, your sister or your friend. Maybe they were the only person that got you. And what does God sometimes do? He permits their exit from your life so you can finally see what amazing things you are capable of with the help of God.

You are awesome, you are amazing, you are strong and powerful, but you will never really know that unless you see your strength apart from others. It has to come from within. While you're thanking God for every person He has divinely placed in your life, remember it is through the help of God that nothing is impossible for you.

Prayer: *Father, thank You for speaking into my heart by Your Holy Spirit. My inability only confirms Your supernatural ability. What I feel I can't do, Your strength will help me do it. Thank You for encouraging my soul. In Jesus name, Amen.*

Unless You Had Believed

"I had fainted, unless I had believed to see the goodness of the LORD in the land of the living."
Psalm 27:13

What would have happened to you unless you had believed? Where would you be right now if you had not believed in Jesus and received His love in your heart? What road would you have gone down if you hadn't believed God had something better planned for you? We shudder at the thought of where we would be had it not been for Jesus. If your believing brought you this far, it is your believing that will carry you on to the other side of glory!

You may have come through the fire and come through the flood. You may have thought, "I don't know how I'm going to survive this!" But you're still here and you are still standing by the sheer mercy and grace of God. Sister, even if you are holding on by the tip of your fingers. Even if you have to reach deep down and pull up every little bit of strength you can muscle. Even if you have no other words to say, but "Jesus!" God sees you and He will strengthen you. "I know your works."

God says, "Behold I have opened a door before you and no man can shut it. For you have a little strength. You have kept my word and have not denied my name (see Revelation 3:8)." While others may have lost confidence in you. They may be discouraged by everything you are going through, but not God. He believes in you. He has faith in the finished work of Jesus. You are His masterpiece and He will complete the work He started in you. God will be glorified in your life! You just keep on believing! You will see His muscle and you will see His glory manifested for you!

Prayer: *Thank You God. You know exactly where I am. You are my God and I am Your daughter. You gave me a heart to believe and it is that believing that is keeping me. Thank You for never letting me go. Thank You for Your mercy and grace. Thank You for loving me the way You do. I believe in You. I trust You. Be glorified in me. In Jesus name, Amen.*

Treasure This Moment

*"Rejoice in the Lord alway: and again I say,
Rejoice"* Philippians 4:4, KJV.

⚜

By the grace of God, you made it to a new day. You are truly blessed! Before you begin filling your schedule with plans and things to do, treasure this moment. Breathe in the goodness of God. Feel the Lord smiling on you. Feel His love. See His hand upon your life and stand in total awe of Him. Tell your cares and worries "goodbye" because God is at the helm of your life, and He is steering you to His expected end for you.

There is so much excitement in heaven over you because this is your time of wholeness, rejuvenation, refreshing and due reward. God is not a hard taskmaster that is all about work, productivity, quotas and counts. He gets pleasure when His children are happy, satisfied in Him and joyful, not only because we know Him, but because we have received from Him what He has promised. Treasure every moment God gives you. Stay in His grace and receive understanding from every challenging life lesson. If you must resolve to do anything, resolve to surround yourself with what you love, surround yourself with who you love, and enjoy your life.

Prayer: *Father God, I love You. I am so blessed to have this intimate relationship with You. Thank You for the gift of life. I receive Your love, Your rest and Your reward. I trust You with my heart and with my life like I never have before. Be glorified in me. Make this time of my life breathtakingly gorgeous. In Jesus' name, Amen.*

Immeasurable Faith

*"You don't have enough faith," Jesus told them. "I tell you
the truth, if you had faith even as small as a mustard seed,
you could say to this mountain, 'Move from here to there,'
and it would move. Nothing would be impossible."*
Matthew 17:20, NLT

♔

We often read about the faith of persons in
the Bible as if it were something
unattainable by us today. But is it really? We
serve a God whose power is unmatched by
anything in this universe or beyond it. We
are admonished that if we have faith, we are
able to speak to the mountain, tell it to
move and it will be removed. It doesn't take
ground-shaking or earth-breaking faith to
accomplish such a feat. The Bible tells us, it
only takes faith the size of a mustard seed to
do so.

In many areas which are prone to
experience earthquakes, the Richter
magnitude scale is used to quantify the
energy released by a quake. Seismic waves or

undercurrents that travel through the Earth's layers are measured by a seismometer to determine the power of the earthquake. Unlike earthquakes, our faith is not measured on a Richter scale. The size of faith that we need has already been quoted by Jesus on the Jesus-scale. Jesus told the disciples, if you have faith the size of a mustard seed, you can speak and move mountains.

Whatever you are believing God to do in your life and the lives of your loved ones, remember your faith has already been measured on the Jesus-scale. Do not doubt it or try to guess its strength. Simply extend your faith and exercise it. Jesus is able to detect it no matter how faint it is or you may be. Because He has all power, He can and will act upon it.

Prayer: *Our heavenly Father, help me to increase our trust in You that my faith may continually be strengthened. In Jesus name, Amen*

Faith Will Allow You to Let God Take Over

"Yet he did not waver through unbelief regarding the promise of God, but was strengthened in his faith and gave glory to God..." Romans 4:20, NIV

Have you ever found yourself in a situation where God is telling you to do something but you're too afraid? After all, you're accustomed to the life you live and you're comfortable. But, you aren't growing. And now, God is asking you to move. To give it all up and walk toward something better that He has planned for you. You'll have to sacrifice some things you want to keep.

Some people might even think you're crazy because the vision you have doesn't look like what they'd expect of God. You may also have to willingly walk into a situation where it would be impossible for you to succeed unless God comes through!

For the first time in your life, you may have to put everything on the line and believe that God will carry you.

But you won't be able to do it without faith. Your faith in God is the very thing that will allow you to let go, and let God take over. You'll have to have faith that although God is removing certain things from your life, He will replace them with things that are greater. You'll have to have faith that while you may not have support in the natural, you will have abundant support from the Holy Spirit.

One of God's many promises is that He will take care of you in all circumstances. He will never lead you where His grace cannot protect you. Whatever God is asking you to do today, have faith that He has your best in mind.

Prayer: *Dear Father, I know that You love and care for me. Help me to hand my life over to You in faith that You know what's best for me. Forgive me for being afraid when I don't recognize what You're doing. Comfort me and cover me with Your love. In times of doubt, remind me that You will never lead me astray. Increase my faith in Your will and promises. In Jesus' name, Amen.*

Your faith in God is all you have.

"Looking unto Jesus the author and finisher of our faith..." Hebrews 12:2

Your faith in God is all you have. It's the core of who you are. The enemy will stop at nothing to cause you to doubt what you know in your heart to be true. If you miss the mark, the enemy will want you to question God's love for you. If you suffer financially, his goal is to get you to question that God is your Provider. If he attacks your physical health, he wants you to question God's willingness to heal you.

Whatever area the enemy is attacking in your life that is the area he wants to cause the most confusion, doubt and unbelief. But you can turn things around with your steadfast faith in God. Your faith is indeed powerful! If the enemy is working overtime to destroy it, he sees it's value. You must understand the precious value of your faith in God and begin to strengthen it. Work it as if it's a muscle. God doesn't want perfect people, He craves perfect faith. The Bible says in Hebrews 11:6, "But without faith it is impossible to please him: for he that cometh to God must believe that he is, and that he is a rewarder of them that diligently seek him." Do you believe that?

You will go through the storm, yes, but your faith will get you through to the other side. Yes, it will! Your faith in God is what holds you together when everything around you is falling apart. Trust that God initiated your faith and He will bring it to full maturity.

Prayer: *Father God, I receive Your words into my heart. Activate my faith by Your Holy Ghost and bring my faith to full maturity. In Jesus name, Amen.*

(Read Hebrews 11)

A message from God's heart for you.

"Call on Me, daughter, and I will answer you. I will give ear to you and hear your prayer. I will show you the wonder of My great love. I will save you by My right hand. Yes, I will keep you as the apple of My eye; and hide you in the shadow of My wings. I am the Lord your God and I go before you in strength and I come behind you as your rear guard. I am your strength. I am your Rock, your Fortress, your Deliverer. I am your God, in whom you take refuge. I am your Shield and the Horn of your salvation, your Stronghold. Call to Me, I Am worthy of your praise. I Am mighty to save. I reach down from on high and take hold of you and draw you out of deep waters. I alone rescue you from your powerful enemy that is too strong for you. I am your support when you are confronted by your enemies. I bring you out into a spacious place; I rescue you because I delight in you."

Prayer: *Father God, we call upon Your Name! We call upon Your strength! We call upon You as our Refuge, our Rock, our Deliverer, our Shield, and our Salvation. We declare that we have nothing to fear because You are our stronghold. You have everything under control, and we will trust in You. In the Name of Jesus we pray! Amen*

(Read Psalm 17: 6-9; Psalm 18: 1-3,16-19)

You can't force love.

"Keep me as the apple of your eye; hide me in the shadow of your wings." Psalms 17:8, NIV.

♔

When it comes to love, you want the kind that comes naturally, not love that is forced. Maybe there's someone in your life that you love a great deal, but they don't feel the same way you do.

The thoughts in your mind may say, "I can make them love me. I can change and become whatever they want me to be. I can change careers, change my hair, get plastic surgery, have their child, leave everything I know and change the way I behave. They will love me; I just have to..." You shouldn't have to change yourself to get love. If God loves you just how you are, anyone He sends your way will also love you just how you are.

At the heart of real love is acceptance. Anything you have to change to get, you will have to constantly change in order to keep.

Love is most beautiful when it is unforced and not manipulated. Let love happen by God's divine orchestration. Whatever He sends your way He will give you the grace and wisdom to handle. You may not be the apple of someone's eye just yet, but you are surely the apple of God's eye. You may not have a David Jonathan kind of friendship just yet, but you have one with God. He loves you in every state and in every season. He took off His priestly garments and wrapped you in robes of righteousness. You will never be able to reach the bottom of God's love for you!

Until someone can love you even remotely close to that kind of love, honey they don't deserve you.

Prayer: *Father God, thank You for speaking to my heart. I know You love me. Help me know it in a deeper way. Deal with the deeper fears in me and shine your light on every false view I have of myself. I deserve real love and I trust You. In Jesus Name, Amen.*

How do you know you are blessed?

"Blessed be the God and Father of our Lord Jesus Christ, who hath blessed us with all spiritual blessings in heavenly places in Christ."
Ephesians 1:3

How do you gauge whether or not you are blessed? Do you look at all of the possessions you've acquired and say to yourself, "I am blessed." Or do you look at everything you lack and say, "Why am I not blessed?" Don't use material possessions or the lack thereof as a gauge for whether or not God has blessed you. You are blessed because you know the Lord.

The Bible says you have received all spiritual blessings in heavenly places in Christ. What are these spiritual blessings? According to Ephesians 1:3-12, you are chosen in Christ, adopted by Jesus unto

God Himself, accepted in the beloved, redeemed through the blood of Jesus, forgiven of sin, you have been given access to an abundance of wisdom and understanding, you have been made to know the mystery of God's will, and have received a rich inheritance in Christ. You are blessed!

Receive and treasure what you have been given spiritually and you will give God access to manifest Himself in your natural life. Solomon understood this principle and requested wisdom, which is a spiritual blessing. God was so pleased with his request that he made him both the wisest and the richest man on earth.

Prayer: *Father, I receive every spiritual blessing You have given to me in Christ. Help me stay mindful to maintain this right perspective. In Jesus Name, Amen.*

He will get you back on track.

"Who hath saved us, and called us with an holy calling, not according to our works, but according to his own purpose and grace, which was given us in Christ Jesus before the world began."
2 Timothy 1:9

Have you ever felt as though your life had taken a drastic turn and you felt nowhere near where God wanted you to be? You can feel too late, too lost, too slow, and like you have lost too much time. Many of us know that feeling all too well, but be encouraged and be comforted.

No matter where you are in life, you have a purposed destination that God is getting you to. If you are still breathing and are still alive, God is at work. You may have taken many wrong turns, but God in His infinite wisdom, knows how to get you where you need to be. You are never too lost for Him and never out of His reach. Because He loves you, He will get you back on track. If He has to move someone out of your way, completely change your environment, greatly strengthen you, and give you undeserved favor in a situation, He will make sure you get where He wants you to be. His power is greater than anything you can ever imagine.

Don't underestimate His love for you. It's because He loves you that He is unwilling to see you die outside of His purpose for your life. You will rest in His love. You will experience His grace. You have not lost too much time to see His promises fulfilled in your life. So don't get accustomed to that lost feeling. Things are about to change for you, and you're going to have to get acquainted with being right where you are supposed to be. Don't worry and don't fret.

God is going to teach you how to navigate through life and how to live totally dependent on the guidance of His Holy

Spirit. He has you and He's not letting you go until you fulfill your purpose and become all that He thought of when He was creating you.

Prayer: *My God. Thank You for ministering to me in such a special way. I love You so much. You know where I am in life and how to get me where You want me to be. I come against all feelings of hopelessness. You are my hope and my confidence. Have Your way in my life. I yield to You and I trust You. Thanks for finding me, for taking me by my hand and escorting me into Your perfect will for my life. In Jesus Name, Amen.*

Lord, Reset Me

"In his kindness God called you to share in his eternal glory by means of Christ Jesus. So after you have suffered a little while, he will restore, support, and strengthen you, and he will place you on a firm foundation." 1 Peter 5:10, NLT

On many technology devices there is a small reset button, that when pressed, restores the device to it's original factory setting.

There are seasons and times in our lives when we get so far from God's original plan for our life. We add onto our life assignments, relationships, and tasks in the same way we load apps onto our phone. We complicate our life with what God never intended to be in our life. And when life gets to be overwhelming, complicated, and frustrating, we know it's time to press reset.

Let God restore you to your original place in Him. Let Him reestablish, resettle and reconfirm you. Let God reset you.

Prayer: *Oh Lord, my life has gotten away from Your original plan. I've added projects, relationships, tasks to complete, and all this stuff to my life that You never told me to add. Now I'm overwhelmed and frustrated. Your grace is in Your plan and I know when I stay with your plan there's grace and peace. Lord, I pray You reset me. Bring me back to my original state and place in You. Reset my heart and breathe Your life into me today. In Jesus Name, Amen.*

Better Than an Ocean-View

"The Lord is my shepherd; I shall not want. He maketh me to lie down in green pastures: he leadeth me beside still waters. He restoreth my soul..."
Psalm 23:1-3a

♔

You may feel like the only way you can truly rest is if things were quiet around you and if you were somewhere on a beach. If you were standing near an ocean on a tropical island surely your soul would be nourished and you would have the strength to go on. While it is a known fact that getting away to a beautiful place helps us relieve stress and feel a sense of peace within ourselves, the truth is, God's presence is better than an ocean-view any day.

Renew your mind to the truth that the same God that created the beautiful and spectacular destinations on the earth is the same God that lives on the inside of you. When you draw near to Him, He expects you to draw from Him. You are never suppose to leave His presence uneasy and not comforted. No matter your current surroundings, you must draw near and draw from His life source within you.

He will calm your fears and restore the vitality of your mind, will and emotions. He will put your mind at ease and lead you beside still waters. He will fill you with peace and quiet you with His love, giving you assurance that He is in control and it is safe to trust Him. The truth the enemy doesn't want you to ever know is that God's spirit is an amazing well of salvation within you. And if he can make you feel as though you need to getaway to have peace, he has you.

Approach God's presence as though you are standing next to a vast ocean, expecting His presence to do for you more than an ocean would. Draw by faith from the deep well within peace, joy, and wisdom. Experience your Savior and very Present Help in a way that you never have before.

He is better than an ocean-view.

Prayer: *Father, help me get this understanding deep in my heart and never forget it. You are better to me than any destination I can go to. I steal away and draw near to you in my heart and by faith I draw from your life within me peace. Quiet my soul. I believe your presence can do greater in me than anything or anyone else can. Thank you Lord.*

A message from God's heart for you.

꩜

"My beautiful daughter, you are My precious girl. I love you with an everlasting love. I have called you, and you belong to Me. There is nothing and no one who can take you out of my hands. You are mine. I have promised you that I will go before you, and I will. I have promised you that I will never leave your or forsake you, and I won't. I have told you that you can trust in Me, and you can. You see, I am incapable of lying. My very nature is Truth. My very heart is Love. I cannot promise something without fulfilling it. Every promise I have given you, is True and is going to happen. I am not slow as some think of slowness. I will make all things new and beautiful, just wait and see. This trial you are in is temporary, and is nothing compared to the greatness that awaits you when you see my face. I know that your heart is hurting today, but take heart My sweet girl – the morning awaits you. Darkness only lasts for so long. Light always breaks through the darkness, and the dawn brings with it a new joy. You are Mine. Sing a new song today sweet girl. Sing a new song. A song of joy. A song of peace. For no other reason than YOU ARE MINE and I love you."

Oh Lord! The message you have delivered to my heart is one I am so in need of declaring and clinging to in my own life. Thank you that you are a God who speaks! Thank you that you are a God who keeps promises! Thank you that your word is Truth and by Truth we shall be set free! I lift up every woman who reads these words Lord, and I pray that she will receive them as I have, directly from your heart to hers. In the mighty name of Jesus pray! Amen

(Jeremiah 31:3, Isaiah 42:6, 1 Peter 5:10, Deuteronomy 31:6, Exodus 23:20, Deuteronomy 1:33, Titus 1:2, 2 Peter 3:9,

Psalm 30:5, 2 Corinthians 4:17, Psalm 33:3, John 10:29, Ecclesiastes 3:11)

Go and Stand By Your Man

"Two are better than one; because they have a good reward for their labour." Ecclesiastes 4:9

While standing near the dinner table, I see my husband with his head laid on the table. I'm feeling frustrated and angry. He is feeling frustrated as well. I hear thoughts from the enemy telling me I am better off alone. The enemy sounded like the rants of an angry and bitter person who is miserable and wants me to be lonely and miserable too. But in the midst of all the emotions going on within me, I hear God's still small voice say, "Go and stand by your man." So I go and stand by him and we hold each other at our side.

As I stood there next to him, a renewed love for him fills my heart and washes over me like a tidal wave. He is my man and even though he has flaws and weaknesses that frustrates me, he is mine. I decided in that moment that I will stand by him for the rest of our lives. This one move alone caused every voice of the enemy to immediately silence and the voice of the Holy Spirit to be heard loud and clear.

In every home the enemy is seeking to divide and conquer. He is busy trying to cause people to stand against each other instead of with each other. He appeals to our emotions and if we don't know how he operates, we will let him turn a small problem into a really big issue. Hear God's wisdom today. Don't give room to the devil.

Stand by those you love. Yes, they may have flaws, but so do you. Work through issues together and let nothing and no one divide you and cause you to stand on opposite sides of each other. You are stronger together than you are apart.

Prayer: *Father, thank You for Your wisdom. I pray for marriage and family, that You will comfort and strengthen us like only You can. Help me to stand no matter what. I plead the blood of Jesus over my family, and I bind the enemy and put him under my feet. He will not divide and conquer my home. I receive Your practical wisdom and choose to walk in it. In the Name of Jesus, Amen.*

Quiet Beauty

"For we are God's masterpiece. He has created us anew in Christ Jesus, so we can do the good things he planned for us long ago." Ephesians 2:10, NLT.

It doesn't matter where you are on your journey, God is at work in your life. You may feel discouraged, but that doesn't change who you are. You may feel forgotten and abandoned, but that doesn't change who you are. You may feel bitter and resentful, but that doesn't change who you are. You are God's workmanship, created in Christ Jesus, so you can do the works, the good things that God preordained, planned beforehand and chose you to do.

You are a quiet beauty
with inner grace
the love of God shines
upon your face
you are drenched with love

deeply enriched
even when you are weak
Sister, you are strength
alone no never
you are God embraced
His glory is seen
even in your mistakes
a servant's heart
God fills your heart
you are His beautiful
work of art
His masterpiece
truly one of a kind
treasured by God
you are His prize
an amazing praise
both tested and tried
and though it's been rough
Lord know's it's been tough
God is with you
for Sister you are
a quiet beauty
with inner grace
and the light of God shines
upon your face

Prayer: *Thank You Father! Thank You for speaking to my heart. Thank You for reminding me of who I am in You. Embrace me. Bless me. Hold me. Love me. Help me. Fill me. Shine on me. In Jesus' Name, Amen.*

Put Your Prayers in Past Tense

"...And Jesus lifted up his eyes, and said, Father, I thank thee that thou hast heard me." John 11:41

⚜

Jesus' words gives us wonderful insight into how to receive from God. Right before commanding Lazarus to rise from the dead, Jesus thanked God His Father that He had already heard Him. God has already heard you. Already healed you. Already given you everything you need that pertains to life and godliness. Thank Him for what He has already done. Your situation will stay in your present until you begin to push it in the past.

Some of us pray, "Lord, give me strength" as though God has left you strengthless. Know that He is with you and He is within you, therefore, you always have strength whether you feel strong or not. Since we have it, we can receive it by faith.

We must practice receiving from God what we already have.

One day I was in desperate need of wisdom. Instead of praying, "Lord please give me wisdom regarding this situation." I remembered what the Holy Spirit had taught me, and I said "Lord I thank You that You have given me wisdom in this situation. I receive it now by faith." Immediately wisdom began to flow.

The eyes of faith are always seeing the end from the beginning. What God did in the beginning for you will determine your outcome. We are called to live by faith, not by what we see, hear, taste, touch, or feel. We must live by what God has said in His Word. We can appropriate by faith every redemptive right and any blessing God has provided by thanking God for what He has already done.

Prayer: *Father, You are my God and I am Your daughter. Thank You for teaching me how to receive from You. Thank You that You have heard me, You have healed and delivered me, and You have given me strength and wisdom. Thank You for helping me push everything I see in front of me, into the past, and walk in the victory I have in Christ. In Jesus' Name, Amen.*

Don't Be Overcome By Repeated Attacks

"So shall they fear the name of the LORD from the west, and his glory from the rising of the sun. When the enemy shall come in like a flood, the Spirit of the LORD shall lift up a standard against him."
Isaiah 59:19

Did you know a device of the enemy is to attack back to back? You can have a season of peace where everything is going well, then you notice one thing happens, then another, and another. It's manifold temptations that are designed to get you out of faith. If you don't understand this tactic of the enemy of repeated attacks, it can throw you off. But thank God when the enemy comes in like a flood in that way, God lifts up a standard against him. The power of the Word of God is that standard. It is your deliverance.

If you know that God delivered you before, He will deliver you again. If He provided before, He will provide again. No weapon formed against you will prosper.

Instead of saying, "If one more thing happens, I'm going to lose it!" Because one more thing is likely to happen. Let the whole kingdom of darkness know, "No matter what happens in my life, I'm going to keep on standing on the Word of God! I'm going to keep trusting in my God! I'm going to keep my mouth full of praise and I'm not backing down for nobody! No matter what it looks like in my life, I have the victory through Jesus!"

Prayer: *Father, I thank you for your supernatural encouragement. It gave me the boost I need to keep moving forward despite temporary circumstances. You are my God and I thank you that no matter what comes my way, you are faithful to lift up a standard in my life. In Jesus' Name, Amen.*

(Read Job 1:1-2:10)

Fight to Believe

"Fight the good fight of faith, lay hold on eternal life, whereunto thou art also called, and hast professed a good profession before many witnesses."
1 Timothy 6:13

According to Vine's Expository Dictionary of New Testament Words, the word "fight" means to contend in the public games, to engage in conflict, metaphorically to contend perseveringly against opposition and temptation, to strive as in a contest for a prize, straining every nerve to attain to the object, to put forth every effort, involving toil, to wrestle earnestly in prayer.

Anything worth having is worth fighting for. And nothing is worth more than laying hold on eternal life, that wonderful prize of the high calling of God in Christ Jesus. It is not received without a fight, without contending, without standing against opposition, enduring trials and tribulations, and passing all manner of tests. We are in a battle and the enemy will stop at nothing to try to steal, kill, and destroy our lives, our vision, our families, and our souls, but we have the victory and we overcome through our faith. If you think the enemy is just going to sit back and let you lay hold on God's promise for your life without a real fight, you are sadly mistaken. Everything, including the kitchen sink, will be thrown at you the moment you choose to believe God's Word and act on it.

When everything has been unleashed against you, the Holy Spirit will teach you how to fight! Your weapons are spiritual, not fleshly. Until the fight is over, you will be in a war against your faith, but it's a good fight for a Kingdom cause. Let your faith in God and His Word, be the wind behind you that propels you forward.

Prayer: *Father God, I believe You are real. I believe Your Word is true. I believe You are on my side and that I have the victory through Christ. No matter what I am facing right now, I know I'm not facing it alone. You are with me. You live within me. You are for me. Teach my hands to war. Teach me how to run in such a way that I will. Be glorified in me. In the Name of Jesus, Amen.*

A Call To Prayer

"I exhort therefore, that, first of all, supplications, prayers, intercessions, and giving of thanks, be made for all men; For kings, and for all that are in authority; that we may lead a quiet and peaceable life in all godliness and honesty." 1 Timothy 2:1-2

Prayer magnifies God, focuses you on Jesus, builds up and edifies your inner man, and makes you more sensitive to the voice of God. "Well, I know God hears other people's prayers, but I'm not sure my prayers are getting through to Him." If you have received salvation that only comes through Jesus, you can know for a fact that God hears you when you pray and if you know He hears you, you know you have the petition you have requested of Him.

"Well, I'm not a prayer warrior like others. After one minute in prayer, I always fall asleep." Well, pray with the prayer warriors. A companion of wise men will be wise. Their habit of prayer will eventually rub off on you. Praying for hours may not be what you are accustomed to, but don't focus on the length of time. Hide the clock if you must, pace the floor if it helps you stay awake, but focus in on getting before God's face. "I know it's important to pray, but I never have time. I'm always super busy."

From the time you wake up in the morning to the time you go to bed, the enemy is busy thinking of ways to steal, kill and destroy your life. You are Satan's top priority. Therefore, continual prayer must be your top priority. It's only by God's goodness and mercy that He blesses us even when we haven't spent not one minute in prayer. But we aren't to live each day on the sheer mercy of God.

We are to thrive on His grace that only comes as a result of humbling ourselves. "The problems in my life have been going on for so long that I have lost faith in the power of prayer. Seems like the more I pray, the worse it gets." That's exactly what the enemy wants you to think. So he designs his demonic attacks to worsen with every prayer you pray so that you will think prayer is futile and pointless. Don't be deceived! Your prayers are powerful. Pray, pray, pray! You are built for supplication, designed to worship to God, made to intercede and pray always. Choose to accept God's invitation to a continual life of prayer.

Prayer: *Father God, You are my God and I am Your daughter. Thank You that You hear me when I pray. I pray that You continue to renew my mind to the power of prayer. Teach me how to develop a lifestyle of continual prayer to you, not out of religious duty or exercise, but for the right reasons. This world needs prayer and you have built me for the spiritual task. Thank You for giving me such a powerful gift that I can offer everyday of my life. In Jesus Name, Amen.*

For more information about Daughters of the King International Ministries Inc., visit us online at www.dot-k.com.

Made in the USA
Charleston, SC
04 January 2016